CRITICAL ACCLAIM FOR
BRET LOTT'S POWERFUL MEMOIR
OF LOVE AND FAMILY

Fathers, Sons, and Brothers

"What an astonishing book. Bret Lott understands why photographs fade faster than memories, why lost innocence is sweeter than innocence itself, and why every man needs his own garage. *FATHERS, SONS, AND BROTHERS* is a brilliant evocation of that weight that is no weight, love."

—Robert Olen Butler, author of
A Good Scent from a Strange Mountain

"Captures the rough-and-tumble of men growing up, through his honesty, lyricism and eye for the telling detail. Some powerful moments in these essays are also the most emotionally charged, as Lott tries to make sense of an uncontrollable world."

—*The New York Times Book Review*

"A book of small epiphanies, full of love and tenderness, curiosity and disappointment, innocence and guilt, questions and answers."

—Charles Sermon, *The State* (Columbia, SC)

"I suspect that what Lott has written is paradigmatic, a parable of the changes in the way fathers, who are always caught between generations, understand their roles."

—*The Atlanta Journal-Constitution*

"In turn son, grandson, brother, husband, uncle, nephew, and father, Lott uses his vivid, elegant prose to shine the twin bright lights of truth and love on the evolving relationships among male family members."

—*Milwaukee Journal Sentinel*

"When Bret Lott wears his heart on his sleeve, it is a wonderful sight to behold. . . . Tender, funny, bittersweet, and satisfying, *FATHERS, SONS, AND BROTHERS* is a treasure map to what most men keep buried—or at least a visa to those shores."

—Elinor Lipman, author of *The Ladies' Man*

"Bret Lott has a special sixth sense for the ordinary. Every one of these essays rides on strong emotion without ever spilling into sentimentality. Compulsory—but also compulsive—reading."

—Sven Birkerts, author of *The Gutenberg Elegies*

Other Books by Bret Lott

NOVELS
Reed's Beach★
Jewel★
A Stranger's House★
The Man Who Owned Vermont★

STORIES
How to Get Home
A Dream of Old Leaves★

★Available from POCKET BOOKS

FATHERS, SONS, AND BROTHERS

The Men in My Family

BRET LOTT

WSP

WASHINGTON SQUARE PRESS
PUBLISHED BY POCKET BOOKS

New York   London   Toronto   Sydney   Singapore

WSP

A Washington Square Press Publication of
POCKET BOOKS, a division of Simon & Schuster Inc.
1230 Avenue of the Americas, New York, NY 10020

ISBN: 0-671-04176-2

First Washington Square Press trade paperback printing May 2000

10 9 8 7 6 5 4 3 2

WASHINGTON SQUARE PRESS and colophon are
registered trademarks of Simon & Schuster Inc.

Cover design and construction by Rod Hernandez,
photos courtesy of the author

Printed in the U.S.A.

This book is for
—who else?—
the mothers, daughters, and sisters involved:
Barbara, Leslie, and Melanie

The author would like to thank the editors of the following magazines, in which these essays first appeared:

SOUND in *Puerto del Sol*

BROTHERS in *The Antioch Review*

ROYAL CROWN: I and ROYAL CROWN: II
(originally as ROYAL CROWN) in *Creative Nonfiction*

ZEBULUN in *New Letters*

ATONEMENT and MORNINGS in *The Chicago Tribune*

FIRST NAMES in *The Seattle Times*

LEARNING SEX in *The Notre Dame Review*

JACOB in *The Gettysburg Review*

HUGO in *The Bellingham Review*

ALLEGIANCE in *The Iowa Review*

WADMALAW in *The Seattle Review*

All the rivers flow into the sea,
Yet the sea is not full.
To the place where the rivers flow,
There they flow again.

Ecclesiastes 1:7

In the Garage

This is the last room: the garage.

We've been in the new house more than a month already, each day thus far filled with putting away all we own, each day filled with trying to find order in chaos. This is our dream house, after all, the one for which we bought the lot, the one we helped design, the one we plan to see filled with our lives and our children's lives here in South Carolina, so putting things in their just and proper places once and for all seems only right.

We—Melanie, my wife, and our two boys, Zeb, age ten, and Jacob, age seven—live a five-minute walk from the tidal marsh along the Wando River, where these spring evenings we can stand and watch the sun set behind Daniel Island, the sky above us reflected on the river to form a wide and shimmering band of blue and red and magenta, and where we can watch slender stalks of yellowgrass and saw grass and salt-marsh hay sway with the movement of the tide. A ten-minute bike ride takes us to the clubhouse, perched on the edge of the Wando, and the swimming pool there, and the marina, where on a quiet morning you can hear the breeze off Charleston Harbor gently rattle the halyards on the sailboats, the rhythmic metal tap on the masts like some impatient dream of open seas, full sails billowing.

Already there are three forts in the surrounding woods to which the boys can retreat; already there is talk of signing them up for the club's swim team. At breakfast we've seen out the bay window everything from pileated woodpeckers to Carolina wrens; yesterday morning, when I took the dog out to get the paper, there stood a doe in the empty lot next door, only to dart, at the sight of our Lab, for the woods at the end of the street.

We're home.

But the garage. No matter how crisp and ordered the inside of the house, no matter how many empty and flattened boxes piled up outside the kitchen door, a house is not a home, at least in my mind, until the garage has been put together. It's only a rudderless ship set for sail, a freshly waxed and gleaming car up on blocks, a perfectly detailed map with no true North. That's what I think, anyway, though I know that if I were to tell this to my wife, she'd only shake her head, let out an exasperated sigh.

"Men," she'd say.

I sit on the bottom step of the stairs down into the garage and survey it all, this endless mass of material goods we've accrued: a two-car garage piled haphazardly with boxes, yard tools, Zeb and Jake's outside toys and sports equipment; and the camping equipment, recycling bins, bicycles, lawn mower, more boxes. A thousand items, all ready and waiting for me, and though I have no clue as to where to start, still my heart shines at the prospect of the job before me, as though by putting it all away I will become a better husband, a better father, a better *man*.

My father, I know, would have thrown as much of it out as he could. His garage was always a lean, pristine place, and it seems now, on this Friday I've cleared for the express mission of setting up the garage, that throwing things out is the way to begin. Separating the wheat from the chaff, as it were.

I stand, go to the mounds of our belongings on the left side of the garage, and pick up the first victim: an old and holey garden hose I've been meaning to repair for the last year or two. But now the truth rises in me, ugly and incriminating: I'd rather just buy a new one than seek out the pinhole leaks and replace the hardware at either end, and so I toss the hose out the side door, the one that leads off into the backyard. So begins, if in a heartless way, my association with my garage.

My father was a man of few words, and even fewer tools. What I remember of the first garage I ever knew was that it was a dark and windowless place: tar paper and bare studs, open rafters above. This was back in Buena Park, California, in a tiny stucco tract house where we lived from the time I was two until I was nine, and I can remember, too, the small Peg-Board above the workbench at the back of the garage. On it hung one hammer, one hand saw, and two screwdrivers, a Phillips-head and a flat-head. That was it.

Sure, there must have been other stuff somewhere in there, but back then garage paraphernalia wasn't important to me. What was important was that after Saturday yard work, we three boys finally done pulling weeds along the fence in the backyard, my dad would hose out the entire garage, giving the concrete floor a slick sheen, a temptation too great for us. Brad, Tim, and I had no choice but to take turns running as fast as we could along the asphalt driveway, then jumping flat-footed onto that cement, blasting from pure California Saturday morning sunlight into the black garage to slide barefooted as far as we could, arms out like surfers' for balance.

And of course my mother forbade our doing this, hollering from the front porch each Saturday about broken arms and concussions. But my father only shook his head at us, gave what we supposed was a smile, then set about sweeping out the water, his garage once more pristine, every item in its place, we boys sliding and laughing and falling and laughing again.

But when I was nine, my father was transferred, and we moved from Buena Park to Phoenix, a place so strange and alien it might have been another planet: saguaro cactus as decorative landscaping, snakes sunning themselves on warm driveways at daybreak, coyotes rooting through the garbage cans.

And nobody had garages.

Instead, we all had carports, open-air structures under which you simply parked your car. Gone overnight was the sense of mystery about the garage, the dark and cool of it, the bare studs and tar paper replaced with eight painted wooden posts holding up a roof.

Though there were still weeds to be pulled, there was no grass to be mowed; instead people had gravel yards, and my father had us out there every Saturday morning raking the gravel into careful, thin lines while he swept the driveway. Gone were the days of slick and wet concrete, the hose replaced by a push broom. This was the desert; hosing down the carport was a frivolous waste of water.

We lived there until I was sixteen, seven years that saw momentous changes in the life of our family: We three brothers entered our teen years and splintered up, Tim, the youngest, following in my dad's footprints, raking the gravel in a manner that would, later in my life, remind me of Japanese rock gardens; me, the middle boy, burrowing into books and band; and Brad, the oldest, falling in with the wrong crowd, turning rebel, finally dropping out of high school his senior year to join the navy.

I can't help but think that, somehow, this loss of a garage had something to do with it. Back in California, we three boys used the garage as a haven from Mom and Dad, built extravagant forts of blankets and chairs and the grille of our '62 Dodge once Dad got home, the engine warm and ticking beside us. In that garage we rode our bikes in endless figure eights all summer long, passed time in the cool dark; in that garage we gave each other practice swats with the Ping-Pong paddle, the three of us having put on two pairs of pants and three pairs of underwear apiece, all in anticipation of what was to come once Dad got home and Mom told him of how we'd raided the garage refrigerator, had eaten every Kool-Pop and Fudgsicle and even the watermelon that afternoon.

It was in that garage that we became, it only occurs to me now, *brothers*.

There is no *there* there in a carport, no sense of place other than one to park the car in; instead of riding bikes in the cool dark of a garage all summer long we stayed indoors, where it was air-conditioned, and watched *Gilligan's Island* reruns until we could guess the episode before the opening credits were over. We took our swats without the luxury of practices with the Ping-Pong paddle, forced to gauge solo how many layers to wear, Mom too nosy and poking her head into our bedrooms whenever we attempted mock tribunals. We tried building our forts in the living room, but the lack of the engine's tick and the absence of the dangerously sweet smell of gasoline revealed to us the sad truth of our improvised architecture: Here were only chairs, here were only blankets. No wonder, then, we each broke for our own lives.

By the time my father was transferred back to California when I was sixteen, we brothers were as good as strangers: Brad somewhere in the South Pacific on the first of his three SEAPAC cruises, Tim attending the new high school, Shadow Mountain, me the old one, Paradise Valley, this split a result of overdevelopment of the area and the opening of a new district. I was first tenor in the jazz ensemble, Timmy a hack tuba player. We three bore nothing in common, though I suppose, of course, it was inevitable, this splintering up; all of us, for better or worse, grow up and away.

Then, literally overnight, there we were, once again in a stucco tract home in Southern California, though this one was bigger, closer to the ocean. More importantly, we had a garage once again.

Saturday mornings we two remaining boys helped with the yard: Tim with a religious fervor that would later find its release in the opening of his own landscaping business, me with the begrudging attitude of the unjustly persecuted. I was a sixteen-year-old who only wanted to live back in Phoenix, where his friends were, no matter the carports or gravel yards. While my dad, oblivious as far as I could tell, only hosed out the garage.

I was a hayseed from Phoenix dropped square in the middle of the surf capital of America: Huntington Beach, California. Timmy was now at the same school with me, though I acted as though I didn't know him, a freshman. I still wore bib overalls and flannel shirts just like everyone else back at Paradise Valley, even when I was surrounded by longhaired blond surfers, male and female alike, wearing Hawaiian shirts turned inside-out, corduroy shorts, and thongs. Timmy took on that disguise with ease, shucking his overalls for colorful rayon hula girls and those shorts in a move that further distanced him, the traitor, from my peripheral vision. Finally band, my refuge back in Arizona once we boys had made our split, turned its back on me: I couldn't even make the band at Huntington Beach High because, the director quietly explained to me my first day there, their jazz ensemble was going on tour the next month, and everyone had had to sell cheese in order to go, and since I hadn't sold any cheese I couldn't truly expect to be included in the trip to Modesto, now could I?

So my days were spent inside a funk of the first degree, me silent save for the muted grunts around the dinner and breakfast tables, a shorthand of squelched anger at my parents, at my little brother, even at Brad. Nowhere to be seen, he was somehow nonetheless implicated in my getting shafted by the world.

Then one morning a month or so after we'd moved, my father of few words nudged me awake in the predawn dark of my bedroom, and I opened my eyes to see him above me, a silhouette against the light from the hallway, there, in his business suit, briefcase in hand, faceless for the dark. As every weekday morning of my entire life, he was dressed and ready to walk out the door before daylight, and I remember sitting up in my bed, rubbing my eyes, then looking up at him again, wondering what the heck had made him wake me.

"Read this," he said, and handed me an index card.

I took it, then reached with my other hand to the desk beside my bed, put on my glasses. I blinked a few times, held the card so that I could read it in the light from the hallway behind him. On the card was typed the words, "God grant me the serenity to accept the things I cannot change, the courage to change the things I can, and the wisdom to know the difference."

"Someone gave it to me at the office," he said. He was quiet a moment, then said, "He heard me talking about you to one of the guys. Thought you'd appreciate that." He paused again, then turned, headed for the hall. He stopped once he was out there, and now I could see his face, could see his eyes on me, his middle son.

He was the man who'd looked at us three boys lined up on the living room couch in our protective layers of clothes that day we'd raided the garage refrigerator, only to pierce us each with his eyes and say in a voice so strong and solid we'd had no choice but to obey: "Boys. Don't do that again." He was the same man who parked the Dodge just so, one or another of us directing him into the garage like a ground-crewman for a DC-8, him setting the brake and smiling, shaking his head while he climbed out of the car, we three already setting up the chairs, unfolding the blankets.

He was the same man who, on Saturday mornings, worked the hose inside our garage, the man who seemed to smile while our mother hollered, we boys having no choice but to run for the cement, blast from pure California Saturday-morning sunlight into the black garage, then slide barefooted as far as we could.

I looked at the index card, then back at him. I said, "Thanks." I paused, shrugged, a little stunned at this moment of help offered by a man of so few words. "Thanks," I said again.

He gave again what I supposed was a smile, then headed down the hall to the stairs, turned out the light. I lay back in bed, heard a few moments later the slow groan of the garage door as my father pulled it open, a sound I almost never heard for the fact I was usually stone asleep this time each morning. I heard the car start, heard it back out. Then came the same slow groan, the cold twist and strain of metal springs, as he eased the garage door closed.

We have survived. Brad is a carpenter in Sequim, Washington, where he lives with his wife and their two daughters. Tim designs and sells wooden playground equipment, those huge structures you see in city parks all over the country, and lives with his wife and son and daughter not three miles from our parents' house in Huntington Beach. And I am a writer in South Carolina, a land so alien to Southern California and Phoenix, Arizona, it might as well be another planet. I'm still stunned at a deer in the yard next door, at woodpeckers and wrens out the breakfast-nook bay window, at yellowgrass and saw grass and the shimmering face of a river at sunset.

And now, at a little after two on a Friday afternoon, the garage is finished. It's a different garage from that one in Buena Park, the walls here Sheetrocked and painted, the two windows that look out on the front lawn filling the place with light, no tar paper, no bare studs. To the right I've stacked a box filled with bats and badminton rackets and the volleyball net, another packed with baseball gloves and various Nerf balls, Rollerblades, and radio-control cars. Above it all I've nailed a metal rack for yard tools: two shovels, two spring rakes, a push broom, and an edger.

To the left are the boxes of gardening paraphernalia, my wife's obsession: hand shovels and garden hose fixtures, sprinklers and sprayers, fertilizers and insecticides and empty terra-cotta pots, all waiting for her gentle hand. Next comes the electric blower, next to that my Weedwacker, next to that the lawn mower. There sits my toolbox, the small gray plastic one; inside it a couple of screwdrivers, a tape measure, a small socket set.

That's it for my tools. Like father, like son.

I'm planning on building a workbench in here, planning to hang a Peg-Board above it to give a home to those tools. Eventually I'll build shelves in here, too, and place these boxes on them so that on Saturday mornings, after the lawn is done, I can hose the place down and teach my boys the finer points of garage sliding. But not before I buy that new hose, the one to replace the holey one buried beneath the discard pile outside, a pile so high I know I've done my father proud.

It's time now for me to pick the boys up from school,

Melanie having gone for groceries, and I step out of this pristine garage, this newly waxed hot rod finally off the blocks, this map of my life finally given its own true North. Time, too, to make some phone calls this evening: one to Washington to talk to a carpenter, one to a man who designs toys for kids like my own. And one to a man of few words, even fewer tools.

I stand back from my garage, hands on hips, to survey it all, then reach to the garage door above me, take hold the handle, and pull it closed.

Sound

Sunday mornings I got up at five for the paper route, put on cutoffs and a T-shirt, tennis shoes with no socks, and went outside. Monday through Saturday afternoons I delivered the *Phoenix Gazette,* but Sunday mornings it was the *Arizona Republic,* thick and heavy. In the afternoons I could do the route—sixty-three stops—in one trip, my paperbags filled and hung over the handlebars of my bike. But the Sunday paper took two or three loads. I'd inherited the route a year before from my older brother, Brad, when he'd decided he was too old for it. He was thirteen then. I was eleven.

Some summer mornings there would be a snake on the driveway, sleeping there since the night before, when the concrete had still been warm. I'd get a broom from the storeroom around to the side of the house, back behind the carport, then move slowly toward the snake—it was never a rattlesnake, always just some brown snake lying flat on the driveway—and poke it with the handle, push it into the river rocks that lined the drive. Sometimes it'd wake up, squirm away through the rocks and across the gravel front yard. Sometimes it was dead.

Winter mornings the sky was still dark out, not even a hint of dawn coming, only cold desert stars, and I'd have to put on a sweatshirt and coat and hat and gloves and two pairs of socks. The rest of the house slept, winter and summer; this was my job, nobody else's. Unless it rained, when Mom drove me in the station wagon.

There at the foot of the drive were five or six bundles: the news sections and the inserts. Sometimes I did the right thing, put the inserts inside the news sections so that the papers read in order. That way my customers could see the world the way it was intended, from the black square box in the front page upper left corner listing something called *Casualties,* inside it strange abbreviations—SSgt, Pvt1C, Lt.jg.—right through to the classifieds buried in the insert.

But most times I just put the insert, with its comics and Sunday magazine and entertainment sections, on top of the news section, folded it, put the rubber band around it, and laid it in one of the loose and empty paperbags on my handlebars. Then I'd make my first trip, the filled paperbags so heavy I could only point the bike down the street and hope I didn't lose control and steer into a cactus in somebody's front yard.

We lived at 2802 Victor Hugo Avenue, and I rode down the street, threw first to Cameron Haney's house—the kid from a place called Queens whose dad worked for American Airlines as a mechanic. Cameron had red hair and wore shorts with five or six zippered pockets, each filled with rocks the right size for throwing. My dad called him Randy, for a reason none of us could figure out, but my dad didn't call any of our friends by their right names, only made up names and called them that from then on. Cameron ate Cheerios with ketchup poured over them. Tim, my little brother, had seen him do it.

Eric Stine's house was at the bottom of the street, where Victor Hugo curved to the left and ran into Joan D'Arc. Eric was one year older than me, and in Troop 226 with Brad and me. I made certain to get the paper on the porch there, because I liked Eric Stine. When we played BB-gun wars, he took good clear shots, didn't cry when he got hit. And Mr. and Mrs. Stine tipped me a dime each week.

I then turned left onto Joan D'Arc, threw papers on up the street. The development we lived in sat next to a small mountain, sharp black Arizona rock poking up off the desert floor. A small hill sat to one side of the mountain, and the ground leading up to the mountain and hill was part of where I delivered papers. The route in this area was a matter of coasting and throwing, pedaling hard and throwing, coasting and throwing. By the time I made it up to the corner, where Joan D'Arc hit 28th, my shirt was sweated through, my glasses sliding down my nose.

I turned left onto 28th and away from the mountain, threw all the way down to Bell Road, where I turned right and threw a couple houses, then right again and back into the tract, the streets flat and straight down here. I threw to Mr. Morrow, the editor of the local weekly, *Valley News and Views,* his son Tom the one to deliver it every Thursday; I threw to the Machmers, who'd spray-painted their gravel "lawn" a dark green, as if we'd all be fooled into believing it was actually grass in their front yard; I threw to Mrs. Bland, Tim's second-grade teacher, an old woman who had a loud cocker spaniel and who wanted her paper inside the carport on the step up to her kitchen door. She tipped me a quarter a week, so that was where she found her paper, even early Sunday mornings.

By this time my paperbags were empty and I'd head up Captain Dreyfuss, turn left onto Emile Zola, hit 28th again, pedal to Victor Hugo, and coast down to the pile of folded newspapers on my driveway, the breeze I made as I rode cooling me down. In summer the sun was up by now and lit the desert in a yellow light. Victor Hugo was the last street in the tract, behind our house three or four miles of empty desert sloping south and away toward Squaw Peak; beyond that row of mountains, Phoenix itself; and though we'd lived here for almost three years already, I still couldn't believe we lived in the desert, a place where snakes slept on driveways, where people had gravel front yards, cactus instead of trees.

We'd moved there in 1967, my dad given the job of sales manager for Royal Crown Cola by the owner of the Phoenix franchise. He'd been a route supervisor for RC in Los Angeles, had worked for them since 1953. One August evening he came home from work to our house in Buena Park, went to the refrigerator, and pulled out a can of beer. He had on a white short-sleeved shirt and a black tie loose at the collar. He had on black-and-white checked pants, the black horn-rimmed glasses he'd started wearing not long before. He'd played football in high school, had driven trucks for RC before he was made a salesman. The glasses made him look funny to me, him with his big arms and thick neck. I'd been wearing my own glasses, plastic horn-rims that looked like redwood, for two years already.

He stood with the refrigerator door open, that can in his

hand, and said to the room, "How'd you like to move to Arizona?"

We four children were in the kitchen, the three boys having followed him in from the street, where we'd been playing 500 with the Walker boys and Steve Jensen and John Steinwand, who was too old to be playing with us and stayed at bat for as long as he wanted. We followed Dad into the house most times he came home, unless we were in trouble and my mother had warned us we'd be getting the belt when he got home. My sister, Leslie, stood on one of the dinette set chairs at the kitchen sink, washing dishes with my mother.

We boys looked at him, at each other. We had our mitts in our hands and only stood there. Leslie, four years old, hummed some tune while she dipped her hands into the bubbles in front of her.

My mom wiped her hands with the dish towel she'd had on her shoulder. "Bill?" she said.

He said, "Phoenix," and smiled, went to the silverware drawer, pulled out a can opener, and popped open the beer. In this manner, our moving to Arizona had been settled.

Now we lived in a house painted the same color as the gravel in the front yard. A twenty-foot saguaro grew in the backyard. Coyotes sometimes dug through our garbage. We wore cowboy boots to school. We regularly climbed a mountain not a block from our house, a mountain that filled the kitchen window when we stood at the sink.

I had a couple of flat streets left to throw before I'd have to go up onto the streets that contoured the hill and mountain:

the upper parts of Victor Hugo and Joan D'Arc. Those would be last on the route, and then I could coast home, park the bike in the carport, go back to bed.

I threw the rest of the houses on Captain Dreyfuss, on Emile Zola, and along Bell. There was the Browns', and the two Great Danes in their fenced front yard. I'd used to collect from them only once a month or so, always just stood out on the street, the huge dogs barking, until Mrs. Brown came out in her bathrobe and paid me. Then one day I put my hand to the chain-link fence and touched the nose of one of the dogs. The dog sniffed my finger, then slipped his tongue through the fence, gave my hand a big lick. Now I stopped and petted both of them, even on these Sunday mornings, and collected every Thursday night.

There was the Stahls' house; the two boys who lived there, Wade and Cody. Wade was a friend of Tim's, Cody about Leslie's age. Mr. and Mrs. Stahl were friends of Mom and Dad's, and they all got together every other week or so. She was a nurse, he worked for Motorola, and we couldn't understand why they let both Wade and Cody say things like "damn" and "shit" and "hell" right there in front of them. If we said anything like that we were grounded.

And there was the Funks' house, the horse they had in a small corral next to the place. I always pulled oddball desert grasses and weeds from along the foundation of their house when I came by, and fed them to the horse. Then I petted its nose, scratched its forehead, and headed home for the last load of papers.

————

The last stop on Victor Hugo was the house farthest away, all the way to where it hit Bell. This was the Polks' house, and the first time I collected there, it'd taken Mr. Polk a good ten minutes to answer the door.

"Coming!" he'd hollered out; then, "Just a minute!"—nowhere any anger or impatience in his voice. Just words to let whoever it was know he was on his way.

Then the door'd swung open, and Mr. Polk staggered into the doorway. He had heavy leather and metal braces on both legs; his face was wet with the work of getting to the door. He smiled, leaned out the door, and put his hand out for me to shake, introduced himself. He tipped me a dime every week, and he didn't have to ask me to put his paper on the porch. Some afternoons when I delivered he'd be around to his side yard, where he had a glider swing set up, and I could hear him whistling. He whistled more beautifully than I'd ever heard before, vibrato and all, and I'd sit on my bike in his driveway, taking a break from riding and delivering in the afternoon sun, and just listen.

By this time Sunday mornings the sun would be in full swing, that yellow light gone already to dry white, though it wasn't even seven yet. Then I'd push my bike up from Bell onto Joan D'Arc, the street highest up the mountain, and I'd start coasting. All the houses were on my right, the steep mountain to my left; so I didn't have to throw across the front of the bike, had only easy throws down driveways to houses whose roofs were only a little higher than the street. Sometimes a roadrunner would cut across in front of me, or a line of quail, or a ground squirrel, but I didn't slow down: I was almost done.

I threw to the assistant scoutmaster's house, Mr. Penney's;

and to the accounts payable manager for RC, Mr. Van Hoof, whose daughter Paula I had been in love with since fourth grade. I threw to Mark Beck's house, and Rick Graham's, where lived the only dog I'd ever been bitten by, an ugly dachshund I'd put my hand out to one day not long after I'd made friends with the Great Danes. The dog, Bitsy, drew blood.

Then I was at the top of Joan D'Arc. Behind me was the mountain, below me the steep drop of street I saved for last. This stretch of Joan D'Arc lasted about a quarter mile, almost flattening out when it hit 28th down near where I'd started the route. I had four papers to throw on my way down; then, when I hit 28th, I'd turn right, trying not to slow down at all, then go the hundred yards along 28th to Victor Hugo, turn left, and coast right on into the carport, and home.

I pushed off, felt the wind on my face, my eyes creased nearly closed for it, even though I had glasses on. I leaned over the handlebars, fished out one of the last four papers, threw it to my left onto a driveway, the slope down growing steeper, my bike going faster. I reached into the bag, got another paper, threw it to my left, to Steve Noeding's house; then got another, threw it to the right to Mrs. Maranger's house, a widow who tipped me a dime a week and gave me five dollars at Christmas.

The wind grew, whistled in my ears, the handlebars lighter than anything I could imagine after having been so full so long. The bags ballooned out with the rush of air into them, and I reached down, took out the last paper, threw it to my right to the Thomases' house, the last one on Joan D'Arc; and now I was already off the steep street and onto 28th. I sailed my bike to the right and along the road, no cars out this early, my last paper delivered.

Then I leaned left onto Victor Hugo, went down two houses on the right, and pulled into my driveway, braked hard as I headed into the carport, the newspaper bags empty. The plastic strips that held the bundles together, the brown pieces of paper the sections'd come wrapped in, lay on the curb, but I just took off my shirt, wiped the sweat off my arms and face and neck, and went inside. I went to the refrigerator, opened it, took out a bottle of RC like I did every time I finished the route, and downed it. I stood at the kitchen sink, tipped the bottle up, and closed my eyes, felt the cold pop burn down my throat. I brought the empty bottle down, looked out the window at the mountain in front of me, and belched.

The last thing I did each Sunday was wash the newsprint from my hands in the bathroom sink, and I marveled every time at the black rinsing through the soapy water, the gray sheen left in the sink when I was done.

Then I went to my bedroom, pulled back the sheets, and lay down, still in my cutoffs, still sweaty. I shared the room with Tim, the two of us in single beds that'd been bunk beds for Brad and me in California. On occasion Tim might roll over, say something in his sleep. One Sunday morning in January, when I was back in bed before the sun had even cleared the mountains to the east, I'd had an entire conversation with him about a rope ladder he saw hanging from the ceiling. But usually he'd only snore quietly, the sheets bunched and pulled out around him, his face buried in the pillow.

My sheets were always cool, and I pulled them to my chest, placed my hands behind my head, and stared at the ceiling. Only then did I hear the sound. Only after I'd soared down Joan D'Arc and thrown the last Sunday paper and downed sixteen ounces of RC and watched black newsprint wash around the sink, then settled back in bed, did the sound rise up around me.

It was what I waited for, something I thought even more mysterious than a snake on the driveway, than a shooting star above me while I folded papers on a winter morning: the high-pitched and constant flow of sound in the room, right there in my ears, a sound so loud, the house quiet, my body whipped by the work of delivering all those papers, that at times I thought my head would burst with it, and I had to sniff or cough or hum a song just to make sure the world wasn't drowning in all that sound.

I lay there in bed listening to that sound, wondering where it had come from, why it was here, what purpose it served; and imagined that perhaps I was the only one on earth who ever heard it. I thought maybe it was because of all the sound I'd just listened to: the wind shouting in my ears down Joan D'Arc, that sound overwhelming me, so that now I heard the smallest sounds, the highest pitches, like what only dogs could hear, and I wondered what a dog whistle really sounded like.

Sometimes, then, I fell asleep. But most times I only lay awake, waiting for what could happen next, that sound passing through me and swallowing me whole, me that much alone in the world.

Ten years later I would be married to a woman who was ten years old on those summer Sunday mornings in 1970, a girl living in a state named New Jersey, a place I couldn't imagine. Ten years later my father would be vice president of Royal Crown Cola back in Los Angeles, and would be fired for political reasons that mystified me, then hired by Dr. Pepper within a week.

Ten years later I would be fired from RC myself, where I was a route merchandiser, because people were leaving RC to work for my father. "So I told DeSantini, 'Go ahead, fire him,' " my dad would tell me ten years later, after his old boss had threatened him by saying he'd take my job away. "I told him, 'He's a big boy.' You are," he would tell me. And I would be fired.

Ten years later a dime-a-week tip seemed nothing.

And ten years later I knew what that sound was: I'd read somewhere it is the noise blood makes rushing through one's head, and I knew, for better or worse, that there really was no mystery. A snake or shooting star was, perhaps, what I should have held in awe all along.

But those mornings in 1970 I knew none of this, the biggest mystery me and what I heard, the mystery of the feeling of flight as I tore down Joan D'Arc before the world was awake, the mystery of the silence of our house those early mornings, and the angle of the sun in through our bedroom window as I lay there, wondering, filled with what I couldn't know was the sound of my own blood.

Brothers

This much is fact: There is a home movie of the two of us sitting on the edge of the swimming pool at our grandma and grandpa's old apartment building in Culver City. The movie, taken sometime in early 1960, is in color, though the color has faded, leaving my brother Brad and me milk white and harmless children, me a year and a half old, Brad almost four, our brown hair faded to only the thought of brown hair. Our mother, impossibly young, sits next to me on the right of the screen. Her hair, for all the fading of the film, is coal black, shoulder length, and parted in the middle, curled up on the sides. She has on a bathing suit covered in purple and blue flowers, the color in them nearly gone. Next to me on the left of the screen is Brad, in his white swimming trunks. I am in the center, my fat arms up, bent at the elbows, fingers curled into fists, my legs kicking away at the water, splashing and splashing. I am smiling, the baby of the family, the center of the world at that very instant, though my little brother, Tim, is only some six or seven months off, and my little sister, Leslie, the last child, just three years distant. The pool water before us is only a thin sky blue, the bushes behind us a dull and lifeless light green. There is no sound.

My mother speaks to me, points at the water, then looks up. She lifts a hand to block the sun, says something to the camera. Her skin is the same white as ours, but her lips are red, a sharp cut of lipstick moving as she speaks. I am still kicking. Brad is looking to his right, off the screen, his feet in the water, too, but moving slowly. His hands are on the edge of the pool, and he leans forward a little, looks down into the water. My mother still speaks to the camera, and I give an extra-hard kick, splash up shards of white water.

Brad flinches at the water, squints his eyes, while my mother laughs, puts a hand to her face. She looks back to the camera, keeps talking, a hand low to the water to keep more from hitting her. I still kick hard, still send up bits of water, and I am laughing a baby's laugh, mouth open and eyes nearly closed, arms still up, fingers still curled into fists.

More water splashes at Brad, who leans over to me, says something. Nothing about me changes: I only kick, laugh. He says something again, his face leans a little closer to mine. Still I kick.

This is when he lifts his left hand from the edge of the pool, places it on my right thigh, and pinches hard. It's not a simple pinch, not two fingers on a fraction of skin, but his whole hand, all his fingers grabbing the flesh just above my knee and squeezing down hard. He grimaces, his eyes on his hand, on my leg.

My expression changes, of course: In an instant I go from

a laughing baby to a shocked one, my mouth a perfect O, my body shivering so that my legs kick even harder, even quicker, but just this one last time. They stop, and I cry, my mouth open even more, my eyes all the way closed. My hands are still in fists.

Then Brad's hand is away, and my mother turns from speaking to the camera to me. She leans in close, asking, I am certain, what's wrong. The movie cuts then to my grandma, white skin and silver hair, seated on a patio chair by the pool, above her a green-and-white-striped umbrella. She has a cigarette in one hand, waves off the camera with the other. Though she died eight years ago, and though she, too, loses color with each viewing, she is still alive up there, still waves, annoyed, at my grandpa and his camera, the moment my brother pinched hell out of me already gone.

This much is fact, too: Thumbtacked to the wall of my office is a photograph of Brad and me taken by my wife in November 1980, the date printed on the border. In it we stand together, me a good six inches taller than him, my arm around his shoulder. The photograph is black and white, as though the home movie and its sinking colors were a prophecy pointing to this day twenty years later: We are at the tidepools at Portuguese Bend, out on the Palos Verdes Peninsula; in the background are the stone-gray bluffs, to the left of us the beginning of the black rocks of the pools, above us the perfect white of an overcast sky.

Brad has on a white Panama hat, a collarless shirt beneath a gray hooded sweatshirt. His face is smooth shaven, and he is grinning, lips together, eyes squinted nearly shut beneath the brim of the hat. It is a goofy smile, but a real one.

I have on a cardigan with an alpine design around the shoulders, the rest of it white, the shawl collar on it black here, though I know it to have been navy blue. I have on a button-down Oxford shirt, sideburns almost to my earlobes. I have a mustache, a pair of glasses too large for my face; and I am smiling, my mouth open to reveal my big teeth. It isn't my goofy smile, but it's a real one too.

These are the facts of my brother: the four-year-old pinching me, the twenty-four-year-old leaning into me, grinning.

But between the fact of these two images lie twenty years of the play of memory, the dark and bright pictures my mind has retained, embroidered upon, made into things they are and things they are not. There are twenty years of things that happened between my brother and me, from the fistfight we had in high school over who got the honey bun for breakfast, to his phone call to me from a tattoo parlor in Hong Kong where he'd just gotten a Chinese junk stitched beneath the skin of his right shoulder blade; from his showing me one summer day how to do a death drop from the jungle gym at Elizabeth Dickerson Elementary, to him watching while his best friend and our next-door neighbor, Lynn Tinton, beat me up on the driveway of our home in a fight over whether I'd fouled Lynn or not at basketball. I remember—no true picture, necessarily, but what I have made the truth by holding tight to it, playing it back in my head at will and in the direction I wish it to go—I remember lying on my back, Lynn's knees pinning my shoulders to the driveway while he hit my chest, and looking up at Brad, the basketball there at his hip, him watching.

I have two children now. Both boys, born two and a half years apart. I showed the older one, Zeb—almost eight—the photograph, asked him who those two people were. He held it in his hands a long while.

We were in the kitchen. The bus comes at seven-twenty each morning, and I have to have lunches made and breakfasts set out—all before that bus comes and before Melanie takes off for work, Jacob in tow, to be dropped off at the Montessori school on her way in to her office.

I waited, and waited, finally turned from him to get going on his lunch.

"It's you," he said. "You have a lot of hair," he said.

"Who's the other guy?" I said. I looked back at him, saw the concentration on his face, the way he brought the photograph close, my son's eyes taking in his uncle as best he could.

He said, "I don't know."

"That's your uncle Brad," I said. "Your mom took that picture ten years ago, long before you were ever born."

He still looked at the picture. He said, "He has a beard now."

I turned from him, finished with the peanut butter, and spread jelly on the other piece of bread. This is the only kind of sandwich he will eat at school. He said from behind me, "Only three years before I was born. That's not a long time." I stopped, turned again to him. He touched the picture with a finger. He said, "Three years isn't a long time, Dad."

But I was thinking of my question: *Who's the other guy?* and of the truth of his answer: *I don't know.*

Zeb and Jake fight. Melanie and I were upstairs wrapping Christmas presents in my office, a room kept locked the entire month of December for the gifts piled up in there. We heard Jake wailing, dropped the bucket of Legos and the red-and-green HO! HO! HO! paper, ran for the hall and down the stairs.

There in the kitchen stood my two sons, Jacob's eyes wet, him whimpering now, a hand to his bottom lip. I made it first, yelled, "What happened?"

"I didn't do it," Zeb said, and backed away from me, there with my hand to Jacob's jaw.

Melanie stroked Jacob's hair, whispered, "What's wrong?"

Jacob opened his mouth then, showed us the thick wash of blood between his bottom lip and his tongue, a single tooth, horribly white, swimming up from it. "We were playing Karate Kid," Zeb said, and now he was crying. "I didn't do it," he said, and backed away even farther.

One late afternoon a month or so ago, Melanie backed the van into the driveway to make it easier to unload all the plastic bags of groceries. When we'd finished we let the boys play outside, glad for them to be out of the kitchen while we sorted through the bags heaped on the counter, put everything away. Melanie's last words to the two of them, her leaning out the front door into the near-dark: "Don't play in the van!"

Not ten minutes later Jacob came into the house, slammed shut the front door like he always does. He walked into the kitchen, his hands behind him. He said, "Zeb's locked in the van." His face takes on the cast of the guilty when he knows he's done something wrong: His mouth gets pursed, his eyebrows go up, his eyes look right into mine. He doesn't know enough yet to look away. "He told me to come get you." He turned, headed for the door, and I followed him out onto the porch, where, before I could even see the van in the dark, I heard Zeb screaming.

I went to the van, tried one of the doors. It was locked, and Zeb was still screaming.

"Get the keys!" he was saying. "Get the keys!" I pressed my face to the glass of the back window, saw Zeb inside jumping up and down. "My hand's caught," he cried.

I ran into the house, got the keys from the hook beneath the cupboard, only enough time for me to say to Melanie, "Zeb's hand's closed in the back door," and turn, run back out. I made it to the van, unlocked the big back door, and pushed it up as quick as I could, Melanie already beside me.

Zeb stood holding the hand that'd been closed in the door. Melanie and I both took his hand, gently examined the skin, wiggled the fingers, and in the dull glow of the dome light we saw that nothing'd been broken, no skin torn. The black foam lining the door had cushioned his fingers, so that they'd only been smashed a little, but a little enough to scare him, and to make blue bruises there the next day. Beneath the dome light there was the sound of his weeping, then the choked words, "Jacob pulled the door down on me."

From the darkness just past the line of light from inside the van came my second son's voice: "I didn't do it."

———

I have no memory of the pinch Brad gave me on the edge of that apartment-complex pool, no memory of my mother's black hair—now it's a sort of brown—nor even any memory of the pool itself. There is only that bit of film.

But I can remember putting my arm around his shoulder in 1980, leaning into him, the awkward and alien comfort of that touch. In the photograph we are both smiling, me a newlywed with a full head of hair, him only a month or so back from working a drilling platform in the Gulf of Mexico. He'd missed my wedding six months before, stranded on the rig, he'd told us, because of a storm.

What I believe is this: That pinch was entry into our childhood; my arm around him, our smiling, is the proof of us two surfacing, alive but not unscathed.

And here are my own two boys, already embarked.

Royal Crown 1

It begins with a game: Each boy is given a bottle of soda—RC or Diet Rite or Nehi or, if we are lucky, a huge quart bottle of a Par-T-Pak flavor—and the cap is popped off by our dad, standing there in the dark garage with the three or four cases of returns he's accrued this past week, bottles delivered to his customers cracked or half-full or murky for whatever reason and given back to him for credit on their invoice. He told us once, the story legend in our hearts, as good as a ghost story at a midnight campfire, of how one time a customer gave back a bottle of Diet Rite in the bottom of which sat a drowned mouse. Truly.

We hold the bottles with two hands at the neck so as not to drop them, then run across the asphalt driveway and across the front lawn to the curb, where we kneel, carefully tip the bottles, and pour out the soda.

Here is the game: Who can empty his bottle fastest and be the next to receive another bottle from Dad? or, Who can take the longest to empty his bottle without stopping the stream of soda? or, What color will Nehi Grape and Par-T-Pak Lime and RC Brown make?

We watch the sodas swirl down the gutter, watch the colors collide and move and mix, watch the carbonation—though we do not know this word, *carbonation,* call it instead *fizz*—swim up as the soda hits the concrete, colors swirling in this Saturday-morning sunlight in Buena Park, California, colors moving down the gutter toward where, we know, it will finally dribble into the storm drain at the corner six houses down, a trail of colors and fizz that starts, as always, in front of the Lotts' house.

Now the bottles are empty, and we stand up, amazed each time at just what has taken place here: the miracle of all this color—Par-T-Pak and Nehi Orange and Cherry and Grape and Lemon-Lime; the deep, rich brown of RC and Diet Rite—and the fun of doing something that seems illicit: pouring out soda on the ground just to watch it happen.

And the final product: We'll each hold in our hand two cents, a nickel if it's a quart Par-T-Pak bottle, once we take them down to the Alpha Beta for the deposit.

We run back across the lawn, across the driveway, into the dark garage, where we place our bottles into a wooden case there beside our dad, who waits with three more bottles, the caps already off.

It starts as a game when we are boys, my dad's sales route Long Beach and San Pedro and Bellflower and Lakewood, one part of his job to pick up returns from customers along the way, give them credit back on their invoices.

And by the time I am twenty-one, Tim nineteen, Brad

twenty-three, we all work for Royal Crown Cola: me a salesman, Tim a driver's assistant, Brad on the table-set crew.

There is no way for me to write about my life without writing of RC; our childhood, adolescence, and young adulthood all centered on Royal Crown Cola, its logo pervasive in our lives: We played with RC Frisbees, lay out on the beach on RC towels, listened to transistor radios shaped like cans of RC Cola. We wore RC T-shirts, rode bikes emblazoned with RC Cola stickers, decorated our rooms with RC posters. We told time by RC wristwatches, made decorative wind chimes out of RC bottles and our Ronco bottle and glass cutter, caught RC baseballs with blue RC baseball gloves.

But beyond that logo and all these RC toys that filled our lives was the truth of its role: RC was my father's *job*, the one that had him out of the house usually before we were even awake and had him pulling up the driveway past dark most nights— my father beat, his route run, his trunk filled with those returns and the accompanying equipment every RC man had to have: stacks of Point-of-Purchase material like Day-Glo carton stuffers, long narrow strips of paper printed with prices you stuffed into six-pack cartons; bottle hangers, Day-Glo pieces of paper precut to slip over the tops of bottles, these, too, printed with prices; shelf strips, those narrow pieces of plastic printed with the product logo that slipped onto the shelf, identifying where the product sat. There were rolls of stickers, all Day-Glo, printed with prices, or with the RC or Diet Rite or Nehi logo. There were always two or three feather dusters back there with which to clean the shelves and bottles, along with a garvey or two, the metal-and-ink contraptions used to mark prices on bottles or cans.

Nothing but toys, as far as we could tell; and when he opened the trunk each evening to pull out the returns, we boys grabbed up the feather dusters, the stickers, the garveys, and had at it with one another, stamped purple ink numbers on each other's arms or hands or foreheads, shook filthy dusters in each other's faces, peeled off sticker after sticker and slapped each other on the back or took them inside to put on our notebooks or bedroom doors or anything else we could think of.

Toys.

There seemed adventure in this endeavor of our father's as well, as one or two Saturdays a month, once the yard work had been done, and once those returns had been emptied, we piled into the Rambler, his company car, and went to one or another of his stores. There he would park, and we would stand and watch as he loaded what he needed from the trunk into the cardboard case he carried with him into each store: all that P.O.P., a garvey, a few cardboard trays to fill out a display. He pulled out his feather duster, poked the handle into his back pocket so that the feathers gave him a tail. Then he turned to us, gave us each a duster, and told us to follow him. Of course we all put our dusters into our back pockets, too, the flamboyance of the feathers like an emblem of manhood, when we were only a trail of three boys behind our dad.

Inside we owned the place, our towering father leading us down the aisles, certain of where he was going, why he was here.

He nodded at assistant managers, stock clerks, exchanged words on the Dodgers or Lakers or Rams, the grown-up manly banter we saw at home only when Mr. Jensen or Mr. Peterson, neighbors of ours, came over. This was our *father*, an adult, a man; and this was his *job:* to come into a store and talk of sports.

Once we made it to the soda-pop aisle we stopped, Dad surveying and straightening, making notes on the back of a carton stuffer as to how many cases of what he would need to fill out the facings on the shelf. While he wrote we dusted off the product and the shelves. Then, of course, we made the inevitable turn toward one another, and the duster wars ensued.

Without a word our dad would head away from us and toward the rear of the store, we three falling in line behind him, ready for what came next: the back room. Here was pure mystery, pure delight: Once past the steel double doors, doors like those we saw in cowboy saloons on TV, we were in another world. Gone utterly were the lights and shining colors and pleasant smiles of the grocery store outside, replaced by this dark cavern of boxes and boxes, by these bare brick walls and stained concrete floors, by these shouted curses from the same smiling stock clerks who'd winked at us out on the aisle.

Still we followed Dad deeper and deeper into the heart of the back room, wove through and along and around toilet-paper boxes and stacks of empty milk crates and pallets piled high with sacks of dog food and boxes of bleach, until there before us stood the rows of product: cases of RC stacked five and six high, towers of bottles as tall as Dad; rows of product, between each row a narrow aisle only wide enough for one person to fit. The danger of it—all this glass stacked so high, ready to crash down on us—made the adventure even sharper, even better, and we played hide-and-seek inside these dark crevasses, or played tag, or banged the handles of our feather dusters against the bottles to make weird music back there in the darkness, while our father took down case after case, piled them onto a hand truck he'd rounded up from somewhere, then checked off item after item on his carton stuffer, until, finally, he leaned the loaded hand truck back, turned, and headed toward those saloon doors.

Back out on the floor, we squinted at the lights above us and followed him to where he'd left the box of P.O.P. on the soda-pop aisle. Then the work began: As Dad loaded in six-packs and single-quart bottles, filled the shelves, set straight the facings, we dusted and dusted, slipped those hangers over the Par-T-Pak bottles, a hanger on every other bottle, and stuffed carton stuffers into every six-pack, there in the slot for the center bottle.

In this manner we learned the science of sales, the importance of P.O.P., what all this *work* really meant: fun.

My first job was a privilege, I was led to believe, and did believe. A couple of years after we'd moved to Phoenix in 1967, my father having been transferred and promoted from sales supervisor to plant manager for RC, Brad, Tim, and I started spending one Saturday a month at the plant in South Phoenix to wash trucks.

We were given ten dollars per truck washed, which seemed a ton of money, even when we split it three ways. Of course there was no even split whatsoever, Tim still only nine, me eleven, Brad thirteen; as a consequence of our ages and abilities, Brad and I each got four bucks, little Timmy, whose job amounted mainly to hosing out trash from the empty bays, left with only two.

These were delivery trucks, twenty-bay trucks; we had to climb up ladders even to wash the windows of trucks whose cabs were littered with empty RC bottles, wadded-up cigarette packs, cellophane off Little Debbie cakes, wax-paper Whattaburger wrappers and chewed-up gum and anything else a driver might dump inside during the month. The cabs themselves lifted up from the back and folded out and down over the grille to reveal the grime-shrouded engine, there like the giant dead heart of some huge monster. We only saw them this way if one of the mechanics happened to be in on Saturday and working; otherwise, no matter how hard we whined, pleading with Dad to haul back the cab for us, he would not do it. "You'll cut off your arm if you're not careful," he told us every time, this assessment of what could happen making the idea of tilting the cab forward even more desirable.

In order to wash the trucks we had to climb them, sit on the hood or roof with a bucket of soapy water and a worn-out bath towel from home—and I can remember sitting there, up what seemed three stories high, Timmy an ant below me trying to spray me down, me throwing the wet and heavy towel at him, Brad then picking it up, starting in with a keep-away game, me stranded on the roof. No different from feather-duster wars, from stamping a forehead with a garvey.

And at that moment here would come Dad, busting out from inside the dispatch office, taking long strides toward us across the empty asphalt parking lot, fists clenched. "You cut that out!" he yelled, me already with my towel returned, Brad with a Brillo pad, hunched at the wheel he'd been scrubbing, Timmy with the hose in a bay, hosing out and hosing out. "You cut that crap out," he shouted, "or I won't let you come down here anymore. You hear me?"

"Yes, sir," we said together without looking up.

A privilege, he led us to believe; and we believed.

The plant was a series of four or five huge warehouses and the bottling line itself, parking lots for the trucks and salesmen and linemen, all of it stretched over a couple acres or so in the industrial part of town. The buildings were painted a washed-out green, the warehouse roofs were corrugated tin, every square inch of ground had been paved over in asphalt that melted in the summer so that there were permanent ruts left where forklifts and delivery trucks had driven.

Inside the warehouses were pallets of stock four and five high, on each pallet six layers of eight cases, so that the stacks I'd seen in grocery store back rooms back in California were nothing compared to this, were only the big memories of a little kid; these glass towers rose a good twenty-five feet high, almost touched the tin roof. The bottling line was in a building attached to one of the warehouses, and was a complex of machinery into which empty bottles were fed and then washed, sterilized, filled, labeled, capped, and cased up.

Here, in the burning light of Phoenix summers, I had my first *real* job. If the stacks of soda in a grocery store back room seemed childishly small after standing inside the warehouse, so seemed the job of washing trucks once I was thirteen and was handed the job of sweeping the lots at the plant.

Lot sweeper. The job title, of course, explains itself. I was given a push broom, given a lot, and given ten dollars a day plus all the RC I could drink. Mostly what I recall about that job are the blisters on my hands even in spite of the work gloves

I wore, blisters the size of quarters there between my thumbs and index fingers; and the heat, and the melting asphalt. One morning my father would assign me the parking lot next to the sales office, which was a shack beside one of the warehouses painted that same ugly green; the next morning I was given the truck-loading lot, the trucks gone already, even when we arrived at six in the morning; the next morning I was given the inside of warehouse 1, then warehouse 2, and 3, and 4. Then the sales lot again.

By eleven o'clock I'd have gotten some work done, my shirt already soaked through, three or four RC's downed, only to have my father scout me out wherever I was and instruct me on proper push-broom technique: "It's not a *pull* broom," he'd say if he caught me trying to rake trash or dirt or what-have-you from a corner, "it's a *push* broom. You push it." He'd take the broom from me then, give it a few strokes across the pave-ment—careful to give it, too, the obligatory clap on the ground once he'd pushed it away from him, this to loosen the dirt and debris caught in the bristles so that he wouldn't drag dirt right back to where he'd swept.

This was my *job*, the subtleties of sweeping. I knew it was a push broom, I knew you didn't pull it. I knew to clap it on the ground; knew, too, that my dad must've had better things to do with his life and career than to come out here in 105-degree temperatures to direct me through all this. I took the broom back from him once he'd shown me his skill, my eyes never meeting his, my head tilted to one side, me breathing out a sigh as only a thirteen-year-old shown the obvious by his all-knowing father can sigh.

I dogged it out there, certainly, especially in the truck and sales lots, those outdoor skillets where the heat up off the pavement burned through the soles of my boots, where sweat dripped down into my eyes all day long, where somehow trash and dirt accumulated each week as though only to torment me, malevolent drivers and salesmen, I imagined, emptying ashtrays on the ground each day just to watch the boss's son die. Like any kid would, I took my share of soda breaks: leaned the broom against a wall and headed in to the bottling line, where I plucked a cold RC from the endless single file of bottles shuffling along toward the casing machine, the stuff bottled at exactly 42 degrees for whatever secret-recipe reasons. Then, once I'd downed that bottle, I had no choice but to head back out to whatever lot I was working, pick up that broom again, and have at it, waiting all the while for my dad to come out, instruct me yet again.

Yet still, even inside that condescension I felt from my father, even inside all that heat, that sweat, there remained the old feel of adventure, the old whisper of the mysterious in it all. We were the men of the house, Dad and I—Timmy only eleven and running the paper route I'd handed down to him, Brad already a lost cause by then, a runaway twice. He'd shown up this time at my mother's parents' house in Artesia, California, broke and crying, certain only that he would not return to Phoenix. After the summer working with my grandpa as a janitor at Consolidated Film Industries in Hollywood, he came home still the druggie in hip-huggers toking up in his bedroom, still the Jethro Tull and Black Sabbath fiend, still the smart-ass teenager my mom and dad'd hoped letting him stay in California with my grandparents might solve.

We were the men of the house, my dad and I: Each morning he came into my room at five-fifteen, called out my name in the dark, then said, "Time to get up"; we rode in to work together, stopped first at the donut shop on Cave Creek Road, where Dad got a maple longjohn and coffee, me a bear claw and a milk; then drove through the small range of jagged mountains that separated where we lived in Paradise Valley from Phoenix proper, the rocks and sagebrush and saguaro cactus all a deep purple in the pale dawn twilight so that it seemed in those few moments before we fell down into Sunnyslope and north Phoenix as though we were on some alien planet, my father and me tooling around on one of those lunar vehicles we kept seeing that summer on TV.

The adventure was here, too, in the oddball jaunts my dad took me on some afternoons, usually merchandising calls at which we did the same sort of work as when we lived back in California; only now we both had hand trucks and there was no play of duster handles on bottles, no games of hide-and seek, only stocking shelves, putting up P.O.P., marking the bottles with our garveys. No foreheads. Men's work.

One afternoon when I was sweeping clear the sales lot my dad slapped open the sales office door, his hand at his collar, working loose his wide blue RC tie, and called to me, signaled me to follow him into the warehouse. "Going out to Pueblo Grande," he said over his shoulder, the two of us moving past the stacks of pallets, my eyes trying hard to adjust to this dark after the white-hot sky outside. "Truck broke down and we got to cover his last stop." He wadded up the tie, stuffed it in his pants pocket.

On his voice I heard a certain edge I couldn't name; he wasn't angry, I believed, though the situation seemed one about which he couldn't be happy: I'd been to Pueblo Grande before, had been camping out there with the Boy Scouts, and I knew it to be nothing more than a desert outpost, a long drive into nothing and back again.

We made it through the warehouse and out to the truck lot, where a truck waited for us, only two bays filled with product, the thick black rubber cords that held the product fast stretched and hooked across both bays. Without a word we climbed up into the cab, and I watched as my dad started up the truck, gave it the gas a few times, that huge engine right beneath us rattling me in my seat, the gear shift between us shivering as he gave the engine the gas again. He checked his side-view mirror, then looked past me to the mirror out my window, said, "Pull it in a little."

I looked at him a moment, not certain what he was talking about, me still trying to take in this scene, something I'd not seen before: my dad settled into the driver's seat of a truck, settled there like he did this every day of his life—and only now do I know what the sound had been in his voice, that edge: My dad, plant manager, was joyful at being back in the cab of a truck. My dad, back in the saddle, where he'd started all the way back in 1953, driving for the company in California. The old days.

But in 1972 I didn't recognize this joy in him, only wondered at why he seemed to be smiling when all we had before us was a long trek into the desert, the only things to look forward to a hot freeway wind in through the windows, the promise of a cold RC once we got to wherever that stranded driver's last stop might be.

"The mirror," he said, and cut his eyes at me.

"Oh," I said, and turned from him, tugged at the tall mirror until it popped a quarter of an inch or so.

I turned back to him, saw him look at the mirror, move his head a little back and forth, sizing things up. "Good," he said.

He put it in gear, pulled off the lot—leaving behind us, I knew, fresh ruts in the asphalt—and I resolved in that moment to clean out the cab once we got back. I didn't want the trash in here—more Whattaburger wrappers, more wadded-up cigarette packages—dumped on my parking lot.

After work we were united, too, for the drive back home. Every evening we went to a drive-thru liquor store a couple blocks from work, where my dad got a Coors in a freeway bag, and a sack of Cornnuts, me a sack of peanut M&M's to go along with the RC I'd pulled off the line on our way out. I was hot, I was tired, I was drenched in sweat—my hair plastered to my forehead and neck—and it seemed some illicit pleasure, that same sort of pleasure I'd known dumping soda onto the ground back in California, simply to let drop into my RC a single M&M at a time, watch it foam up, then take a sip at the bottle, draw the candy into my mouth, chew it up, while beside me sat my father working on a beer, tossing back Cornnuts, on the radio Tammy Wynette or Porter Wagoner or Buck Owens or Dolly Parton.

I wasn't a kid anymore, I knew. These secret rites that'd passed between us—longjohns and bear claws, beer and M&M's—had ushered me, along with a job paying ten bucks a day, into manhood, even though I was only thirteen, even though I hadn't yet started high school. It seemed a good life, all this cash, all this RC.

But here were those blisters, I remembered, the cold bottle in my hand some small comfort on the white, dead skin, the tender flesh beneath it. And still each day Dad told me how to sweep, felt compelled for some reason to reiterate the numbskull knowledge obvious to me, as though somehow I'd forgotten overnight how to push a broom.

The next summer I graduated to sorting bottles for the line, each morning a couple hundred cases of empties stacked inside the warehouse and waiting for me to sort RC with RC, Diet Rite with Diet Rite, Par-T-Pak with Par-T-Pak, 16 ounce with 16 ounce, quart with quart. When trucks delivered product to stores, they brought back with them these empties; sometimes the stores had sorted them, many times not. That lowliest of line jobs was left to me, the job that involved standing and bending over and simply matching bottles with bottles so that, once they were sorted, the right bottles would be loaded onto each bottling line; no Par-T-Pak bottles filled with Diet Rite, no RC bottles filled with grape Nehi. Each day consisted of sorting a good two hundred cases of bottles, a thankless job and a lonely one—the only person I talked to was the line foreman who tooled around in his forklift all day long, choosing to drive the lift rather than walk twelve feet to attend to some task. On occasion he stopped and admonished me to move faster, but most often only showed up once I'd filled a pallet with empties.

The only other visitor, of course, was my father, who stopped in once a day and bent over the empty cases before me, showed me proper technique: how to hold eight bottles at once, fingers spread, and how to arrange the cases around me so that I could more efficiently fill them with empties. He worked feverishly those few minutes he was with me, his face flushed with the effort, the tie he wore tight at his neck, his hands moving quickly.

That summer Brad was arrested twice for possession and totaled my mom's '63 Buick LeSabre. He claimed the guy in front of him hadn't put on his blinker, and so when Brad passed the guy he'd had no idea the asshole would turn left into him. At the end of that summer he dropped out of high school and left for the navy, my parents signing the papers that said their seventeen-year-old son could join. Timmy still had the paper route.

When Dad finished with my daily instruction, his few moments with me like some sort of RC devotional, he stood up, face flushed, and dusted his hands. "Hurry it up, now," he said each time, and nodded, satisfied.

The next summer I moved up the corporate ladder a rung or two, started out my ten weeks off—the last two weeks of each summer were reserved for marching-band practice at PV—with the prestigious job of loading those empties onto the bottling line itself. There I worked in the cool of the bottling-line building, fluorescent lights above me, people to talk to: Manny, Red, Gonzales, Marvin, a host of others whose names I cannot now recall. I stood at a pallet and loaded those empties into a machine, my old job filled now by a kid named Harlan, the mechanic's son, who knew no other language than that of motocross.

But here I was, fifteen years old and communing with *men*, all of us working together to accomplish a single goal: Get these bottles washed and clean, get them filled with product, get them capped and labeled and sent off to the warehouse, where they'd be delivered up to those stores who sent back empties to be sorted the next day. It seemed to make sense, this endeavor; seemed, even, fun: I loaded cases onto a short conveyor belt that moved the bottles only a few feet away from me, where a huge machine with arms equipped with suction devices, twelve or twenty-four to a case depending on which product we were bottling, descended upon the bottles, pulled them up from the cases, then brought them to the mouth of the machine, where they were shuffled into a single file and disappeared into the raging depths of the next machine down, the washer.

Here the men laughed, here they joked and cursed and spit and cursed and laughed some more. And here I was, my father nowhere to be seen except when he was passing through on his way somewhere else. No more instructions, no more intervention. I was on the line now, couldn't be interrupted with instruction. Here it was do-or-die. So I worked at loading empties; worked, later, at the labeling machine, loading stacks of gummed paper into a round machine that wet each label, slapped it onto the filled bottle passing through, then brushed at the paper, securing the label. I hosed out the floors when told to do so, swept up the glass when a bottle exploded, kept the empties coming. And still my dad did not talk to me.

At lunch I went with the other men to a café on the other side of the railroad tracks that paralleled the RC plant, a white cinder-block place with a flat gravel roof and two waitresses about whom the linemen made jokes every day. Every day I ordered country-fried steak, french fries with gravy, and RC, and paid for it with my own money.

Now I was truly in the ranks, I knew, because of this matter of money: I punched in on a time clock, had my own card, was responsible for not being late back from lunch, and for signing the card. I was making $2.25 an hour the whole summer long, and because my dad stayed so many hours late, the two of us finally rolling home at dusk each night, just as he himself used to come home in the Rambler back in California, I worked more hours than most of the men there.

Each Friday we received our paychecks from the line foreman, who sat on the seat of his forklift, called out our first names, and handed us the white envelopes printed with that RC logo on the top left corner. This ceremony was followed by our obligatory bitching and moaning about how much money we made, and I can remember one Friday in particular when Red, a pale, skinny lineman with a snatch of red hair and a sparse red mustache—a man, I knew, who had a wife and three children at home—pulled out his paycheck and shook his head, in his face loss, somehow, or perhaps disbelief. His eyebrows were up, his mouth barely open as he spoke.

"Seventy-two dollars and sixteen cents," he said, and let out a breath. "Now how the hell am I supposed to live on this?" he said, then folded up the check, put it in his back pocket.

There I was, in my hand a paycheck for $90.73.

Something about this seemed all wrong then, seemed a sham in some way I could only identify as me being here inside the circle of men whose lives depended on this check. I was only a kid, fifteen, whose dad ran the place. I was only a kid and could lay no claim, really, to this huge wad of money in my pocket. I was saving money for a car, was saving money for pizza after football games this fall, was saving money for a new sleeping bag for Boy Scouts. But this man had less than me, and had it only for his family, had it only for food and clothing and shelter.

Once my dad had stopped at the liquor store, the old man at the window just nodding at us, handing through to my dad his beer and Cornnuts, my M&M's, I told him.

"Red made less money than me last week," I said.

He handed the man the money and then popped the beer, but held it to his lips a moment before he took a sip. He pulled out from under the awning to the street, looked both ways. He didn't look at me.

"What the hell, is everybody showing their paychecks around?" he said, his voice, we both knew, too loud for inside the car. He pulled out onto the street, headed for the freeway.

"No," I said. "He just said how much he got." I hadn't yet opened the M&M's, for some reason not sure if I even ought to. But I could see something in my dad, knew he saw in what I was saying what I felt about the whole thing.

Finally he shrugged. He took another sip, placed the beer between his legs; his wrists on the steering wheel, he tore open the Cornnuts. "Just don't tell him how much you made," he said, quieter. "Just don't let him know." He paused, tossed back a couple of Cornnuts. "That's private," he said, and it seemed in the way his voice had gone quiet, in that shrug, and even in the way he paused before taking that first sip, that he'd seen how I felt, this notion I'd not encountered before: work, the truth of a job. This wasn't fun, but a job. How you lived.

I never complained about paychecks after that, only slipped mine into my pocket on Fridays, opened them after I made it home.

Uncle

The story goes that my father and his older brother by two years, my uncle Lynn, hated each other.

Uncle Lynn has told a million times the story of how he could gauge precisely how far my dad could throw (a) a stick, (b) a pinecone, or (c) a rock, and how he used to lead my dad through the Mississippi woods, taunting him, calling him names, egging him on just so Dad'd throw something at him there in the forest.

And every time my dad got mad enough and frustrated enough to play along with his brother's game, the game ended the same: The pinecone or the stick or the rock would land at my uncle's feet, only to be followed up with more taunting, more egging on, my uncle turning and leading my dad even deeper into the woods, hoping he'd throw something just so he could see my dad frustrated, a little boy surrounded by kudzu and wild grapevines and live oak, face red, mad.

Uncle Lynn laughs every time he tells this story, his laugh an open-mouthed one, all his teeth showing, his eyebrows up and high on his forehead, eyes open wide, as though in stunned amazement at how funny this all is. We all laugh, too, when we hear it, we sons of Wilman: Brad, Tim, and me. We laugh when we see in our imaginations our dad red faced and pissed, frustrated. Our dad as a little, angry boy. That's a good one.

The end of the story, though, is the one you hear from my dad: One day, after years of the same old game, my dad smacked his brother in the shoulder with a rock. He'd started growing up, growing bigger, stronger—he would, finally, eclipse my uncle in both height and strength, landing a football scholarship to Ole Miss—and in my mind I see my uncle rubbing his shoulder, stunned into silence not by pain but by progress, by the fact that his little brother, that little fart he thought he'd known, could throw farther than he'd reckoned. This is the story my dad tells. And this is where he gets to laugh. It's the same sort of laugh: open mouthed and loud. The Lott laugh, I guess. But my dad's is sweeter, of course: He gets the last laugh.

My dad was the youngest of three brothers. There were six kids in all: Billie Jean, the oldest, then James, Burton (who would later be renamed Lynn by his pals at the muffler shop where he worked once he'd moved to California), then Wilman, Anne, and Brenda. Brenda was born with Down's Syndrome, and as a consequence my dad's mother, Myrtis, gave her life over to that daughter, made her her favorite not out of choice but love and duty and faith.

My grandma Lott recently passed away, and after the funeral all the family members went back to her house—a bungalow, really, in Redondo Beach. I am curious by nature—*nosy* would be a truer word—and decided to start poking through her belongings, not to try and rustle up something valuable I could lay claim to, but simply to see what my grandma thought to keep of her life.

The first thing I found in the top of her closet was a small wooden box with a metal clasp, and I brought it down, opened it up. In among receipts for electric bills and report cards for Billie Jean and James and letters of reference from the banker and lumberyard foreman and principal of the elementary school, all from when they lived in Mississippi, was a neatly folded square of paper, written on it *Important*, beneath that the word *Keep*.

I unfolded it, the paper brown and worn and creased, to find the following poem in my grandmother's hand, a testament, I believe, to how she felt about having to single out one of her children as a favorite because of matters out of her hands:

ODE TO MY BABY
Myrtis Purvis Lott

You're my morning's blessing and
my night's care.
You're my laughter and my tears, my
sunshine and rain.
A bit of humanity thrown from the
hand of God to fill my days with
love and care.
You're my everything, a blessing
in disguise.

My other babies I turned loose—
and let go.
But you will stay with me always
to brighten and sadden my later
        years.
My everything—
my baby, be of good cheer.
We will live, pray and love
till God comes.

Brenda, then, was her special one, always her baby. But of the rest of the children, it was my dad, the youngest of the boys, who was the chosen one—which, of course, engendered no end of resentment and hostility toward him, to hear my dad tell it, and no end of special treatment, to hear Lynn tell it. James, the oldest of the three, seemed not quite to enter things, just enough years older to be kept out of the fray, except for the time Lynn stuck him in the leg with his penknife on the school bus. Just to see what would happen, Lynn tells it. Other stories involve peeing on one another from upstairs windows, trying to drown one another in the lake near where they lived, even, later, stealing each other's girlfriends away.

But my dad, for instance, got to ride up in the cab of the pickup truck my grandfather drove, while the rest of the kids sat in the bed. He got the first pick of the meat at dinner, got new clothes instead of hand-me-downs. This sort of thing.

Fights, of course, resulted.

In other words, typical brotherly activities. Brad, Tim, and I fought each other in our pool in Arizona, held each other under water for as long as we could; we wrestled in our living rooms, wrestled until we were so sweaty and red faced and angry that Mom or Dad made us stop just when it seemed I might break that half-nelson Brad employed, or just when it seemed I might have perfected that half-nelson I held Timmy in; we had BB-gun wars in the desert: I once shot Timmy in the back of the head from about twenty feet for no good reason other than that I wanted to see what would happen; and we all had to duck when entering Brad's bedroom, for fear he might be shooting X-Acto knives from the barrel of his BB gun rifle at the back of his bedroom door, as was his custom; Brad pinned down my shoulders with his knees and gave tittie-whistles, pinching my nipples hard and not letting go until I whistled; I pinned down Timmy's shoulders with my knees and gave a series of small, rapid slaps to his stomach, hollered out, "Pink belly, pink belly," until he cried; Timmy told Brad, who pinned down my shoulders, gave me tittie-whistles. *Etcetera.*

When I was given my first route with RC Cola, my uncle Lynn rode with me. He was an account manager then, in charge of selling at the corporate level to Vons and Albertson's. My dad was the vice-president. Lynn and I rode together for a week straight, the two of us hunched inside my Datsun B210. He spent the entire week lecturing me, but it wasn't the kind of lecture you groan over, the kind you hope not to be subjected to for hours on end. The kind your father might give.

"I urge you to sow your wild oats right now!" he exhorted me our first morning together, him seated beside me in his three-piece suit, me in my RC uniform. "Do it now, my friend," he said, "because there's going to be a day when you won't have the opportunity or the ability to do so." He'd lost the two middle fingers of his left hand on a machine press when he was a teenager, and it was at this moment he raised that hand and pointed at the air just above the dashboard in emphasis, though he wasn't actually *pointing;* it was just the fact he was missing a couple of fingers that made it appear so. "Only through concentrated effort," he said, and jabbed that hand at the air on those last two words, *concentrated effort,* "can one achieve one's goals. Sowing wild oats should be one of your goals." He jabbed that hand one more time, just to make the point. Here we were in a Ralphs parking lot in Costa Mesa, the sun just up over the palm trees that lined the lot, my uncle telling me to have sex early and often.

"I tell you what I would do if I were a man of your considerable talents and commendable looks, not to mention fine hygiene skills," he went on. He loved to use words, I came to see during that week, and articulated each one so that it sat by itself for a fraction of an instant between us before the next one arrived, that hand once up, up for the duration, cocked like a gun and ready to emphasize. "I would find the most interesting and arresting female individual I might encounter while out running my sales route and endeavor to see what might happen were I to ask her out." He paused, got this grin on his face. Then he winked, said, "Yes-sir-ree," and nodded. "Concentrated effort."

Not what my dad would say. Were he to say anything.

I think it important to note at this point that, while my father had three boys, my uncle had three girls. No boys, and

I think he believed this opportunity to spend a week with a nephew his one moment to dispense all the father-son wisdom he'd been denied dispensing his entire life. So driving between stops was filled with those Boy Stories, the ones about peeing on each other, about drowning each other, about Dad inside the warm cab of the pickup grinning at my uncle through the glass, him huddled with his siblings in the cold while on the way to town.

He told other stories: Once, on a double date, my dad and uncle and two girls all crammed into the cab of that same old truck, my dad had to make a three-point turn on a dirt road in order to head back the way they had come. Dad put his arm on the seat back, suavely, and looked out the rear window to back up. As he gave it the gas, he glanced over at Uncle Lynn, then winked at him over the heads of the girls: *Mission accomplished: My arm is in place.* Then the rear tires slipped off the edge of the road and onto an embankment. Dad panicked, gave it the gas. The truck slid down the embankment before it rolled once, then twice, on down into the drainage ditch at the bottom.

Another time, when the two of them had summer jobs at an ice-cream plant in Columbus, my father had gotten so hot working at stacking crates of ice cream that he'd had the grand idea of simply licking the ice that'd formed on the walls of the freezer he moved in and out of all day. His tongue, naturally, stuck, and it'd been my uncle who discovered him, crying there in the freezer, Lynn laughing a good five minutes or so before he'd finally gone for warm water.

Uncle Lynn moved out to California in 1951, a year or so before the rest of the family. He simply drove off one day, so certain of himself and what he could do. He got work at a muffler shop in downtown Los Angeles, then sent word back to my grandma and grandpa of how good life out there was.

They came, the family whittled down by then to my grandparents and Wilman, Anne, and Brenda; Billie Jean and James were already married, starting up families of their own. The rest, of course, is history: how my father first graduated from Venice High School, then worked at a moving company with my grandfather, then stumbled into a job driving a truck for Nehi, Uncle Lynn following him there from the muffler shop. Twenty-five years later, there they were: vice-president and accounts manager for Royal Crown Cola. Uncle Lynn was divorced in 1971; my parents just celebrated their thirty-eighth wedding anniversary. Uncle Lynn drives a Yamaha 750, my dad a Buick Park Avenue. Uncle Lynn uses words with reckless abandon, while my father abandons them altogether.

Now my two boys are nephews to my two brothers, the older of whom simply left home one day for the navy, so certain of himself and what he could do, the younger of whom graduated high school, then stumbled into a job driving a truck for RC Cola.

Uncle Lynn felt it his duty to tell me stories, reveal to me a side of my father I'd not seen: that episode with the tongue on ice, that slow and embarrassing roll of a truck into a ditch with a girl in his arms. Things my dad would not, I believe, tell me for fear he'd look foolish.

Because what father wants to look foolish to his children? And what other role, then, does an uncle play except to place your father in context, bring him down from on high to reveal to you the red-faced boy with an arm not quite strong enough?

What, someday, I'll tell Brad's children, Allison and Rachel: One Christmas when Brad was about fourteen, he asked for a fluorescent black light to put in his room in order to fully appreciate the Jimi Hendrix and Jethro Tull and Black Sabbath posters on the walls in there. Mom told him not to fear, and told him, too, not to buy one before Christmas. Of course Brad rode his bike to the local hobby shop two days before Christmas and bought the cheapest black light he could find, a little thing no longer than a ballpoint pen, then brought it home, set it up in his room. That was when Mom, furious, disappeared into her room, emerged a few moments later with a wrapped box, and made Brad open it right then, right there in his bedroom.

A fluorescent black light, two feet long and as big around as a baseball bat, mounted on a wood-grain base. Once he'd opened it she put out her hand, and he gave it back to her. "Merry Christmas," she said, and returned it the next day, got her money back on it.

What, someday, I'll tell Tim's children, Clayton and Faith: One summer night not long before school started up—Brad headed for eighth grade, me fifth, Timmy second, Leslie kindergarten —we children were told to try on our new school clothes for Dad. Brad and Leslie went to their rooms, Tim and I to the one we shared. I was quicker on the draw, had on my madras shirt and stiff new jeans when Timmy was still climbing into the pair he'd tried on at Montgomery Ward just this morning. I was the first back to Mom and Dad's bedroom, the two of them waiting there for us.

That was when Timmy let out a shriek, and I turned, startled, to see him, shirtless and bent over, waddling into the room, his face twisted into lines that made his eyes disappear, his mouth a huge O of pain.

He fell to the bed, still shrieking, and lay on his side, curled up and howling. Mom and Dad were right there, standing beside the bed, leaning over him. "What's wrong?" Mom said, "what's wrong?" and put a hand to his face, tried with the other hand to pull his hands from where he'd jammed them between his legs. "Oh no," she said, "oh no," and I saw her turn to Dad, standing beside her. She was smiling, trying hard to hold back a laugh. "Get some ice," she said to me, but I didn't move.

By this time Brad and Leslie had made it to the room, and my mom called for ice again. This time my dad went for it. "Now lean back," Mom said, "lean back so we can help."

Slowly Timmy leaned back on the bed, sort of uncurled himself, to reveal to all of us the sad fact of his pain: He'd caught his penis in his zipper. "Ohhh, man," I let out, and felt myself shrink.

"Shit, man, that must hurt," Brad said, and before my mom could shoot her eyes at him to reprimand him for his filthy mouth, Leslie, headed for kindergarten in a week or so, said, "Shit, man, that must hurt."

Timmy howled, rolled his head back and forth.

Then Dad arrived with a couple of ice cubes, and they started in, icing the poor kid down so they could more effectively loosen the offending teeth. A couple of minutes later the work was done, Timmy released with a newfound caution, one I'm sure he still holds close, even this many years later.

And what will my brothers, my sons' uncles, choose to tell my boys, Zeb and Jake, about me? Most likely one of those stories will have to do with my role in the music program in fifth grade when, bell-bottom clad and tambourine in hand, I had a solo, sang Bobby Sherman's "Easy Come, Easy Go" to a guffawing crowd of elementary-school kids. At least that's the one sticks in my mind. Chances are, though, there are stories they've savored, ones I've repressed, my brothers holding on for just the right day to step into their roles as uncles, spoilers of my paternal authority.

I see my father only once or twice a year now, and each time I see him he's aged a little. I see it in the lines beside his eyes and mouth, the minuscule network of broken vessels across his cheeks. I see the two of them together, my uncle Lynn and Dad, even more rarely; the first time I had seen all three boys together—James, Lynn, and Wilman—in over five years was, in fact, at my grandmother's funeral.

But even on this occasion, the death of their mother, there was still Lott laughter, three men open mouthed and laughing at their own histories, the old stories surfacing again to reveal the same boys they've always been: the penknife, the peeing, the pinecones. The only difference is that now they are orphans, both their mother and father gone, and I couldn't help but feel while watching them laugh in the living room of their mother's

Redondo Beach bungalow that these old stories are what make them who they are and who they are not. Especially in the face of the death of family.

Just as a black light, a rogue zipper, and a Bobby Sherman song distinguish us brothers from each other. Someday Brad will get hold of my two boys, as will Tim. And I'll get hold of *their* kids, my nieces and nephews, and we three uncles will tell stories designed not just to entertain, but to stake our claim to what little territory we have on this earth: who we are.

 Zebulun

This story starts five years ago, back before we bought our first house, back when we were renters in a complex of duplexes. I was standing at our bedroom window one overcast afternoon, the curtains open. The window looked out onto our street, a cul-de-sac, and I was there at the window simply because I'd heard Zebulun out on the street, hollering and carrying on. Only a week or so before, my mother and father had visited from California, and for Zeb's fourth birthday they had taken him to one of those warehouse toy stores, everything from Matchbox cars to huge playpools all stacked to the ceilings. My parents and Zeb were there to buy his first bicycle. With training wheels, of course. He'd outgrown his tricycle a few months before, too often borrowed the boy across the street's Big Wheel. It was time, we figured, for his own bike.

I watched Zeb riding his bike off to the side of the street, almost on the sandy shoulder, as the complex had no curbs. Several yards ahead of him was the boy across the street, Aaron, a year and a half older than Zeb, riding his own bike. More than a year before, he'd outgrown the Big Wheel Zeb so often took over. And twenty yards or so ahead of *him* was another boy, our next-door neighbor's kid, a boy of about eight. He had on a Cub Scout uniform, bright yellow neckerchief over his shoulders, navy blue shirt. He was riding a bigger bike, this one pieced together: outsized handlebars, front wheel smaller than rear, frame the color of rust.

I watched, ready, as any father would be, for my son to fall or for him to weave out into the street and get hit by a car, though few came through here, the end of the street just a few houses down to the right. I waited for something to happen. Of course, nothing did. The Cub Scout, already three houses down to my left, screeched to a stop, left a skid mark behind him. Then Aaron pulled up, put both feet on the ground. The two of them turned, watched my son.

Zeb was hollering now. I wouldn't say he screamed, though he was being loud enough for that word. But *scream* makes it sound like he was terrified, whereas Zeb was a four-year-old kid whose body was so filled with energy, with exuberance, with the joy and freedom found in riding a two-wheeled bike just like the big kids', that it had no other outlet. He still hadn't mastered the bicycle; he pedaled it slowly, his feet not quite used to pushing forward and down at the same time. He wasn't used to using his forward momentum to get the thing moving more quickly, and so, though he was doing the best he could to keep up with the other two, older than he and pros at the subtleties of bicycling, he still had this power, this energy, this *hollering* left in him. Though I could not see his face from where I stood, I knew what it would look like: His eyes would be wide open, the eyebrows as far up his forehead as they might go; his mouth would be open in a full smile, most all his teeth showing, from inside him coming this joyful sound.

I hadn't yet decided what they were doing out there, wondered if they were racing or if they were just goofing around. But then, as soon as Zeb came up to the other two, the Cub Scout wheeled his bike around in the opposite direction. Before Zeb had even stopped his bike, the idea of pushing back on the pedal in order to slow the bike down still foreign to him, the Cub Scout shouted, "Okay, now let's have a race back to the end of the street."

He took off. Aaron, a little bewildered—he looked back at Zeb a moment, then to the Cub Scout, then to Zeb again, as if he bore some fragile allegiance to my son—started pedaling away.

By this time Zeb had managed to get his feet to the ground. He stopped the bike, turned it around in the direction the other two had already gone. He put his feet to the pedals, slowly pushed on them, started moving on down the street.

The Cub Scout was the model of efficiency: head down, rear off the seat, legs pumping furiously. The wind he created pushed back his hair. Aaron was in the midst of imitating him, his bottom off the seat, his feet moving not quite as rapidly. He looked up on occasion, to see, I imagined, exactly what it was that older kid did that made him go so fast.

Then the Cub Scout looked behind him, shouted, "I'm going to win!"

Aaron said nothing, only looked up a moment, bowed his head again.

But Zeb, my son, his brand-new bike beneath him, was

already hollering, already joyful, his feet moving too slowly to let him ever gain on Aaron, much less the Cub Scout. I could see his face now, saw his expression was just as I'd imagined, except that the brown hair down on his forehead was a little stringy, wet with the sweat of exertion in a race he would be doomed to lose every time. In the midst of his shouting, his elation at simply being there and moving, he yelled, "No, *I'm* going to win!"

By now the Cub Scout was at the end of the cul-de-sac, and jammed on his brakes, laid another skid on the ground. My son was just now coming abreast of our house, still had a hundred yards to go. And he was still hollering, still just as happy, still just as filled with the pure, clear glory of pedaling his new bike, of playing.

What he doesn't know, I thought, and an immense fear came over me, a dread of the future, of that day when my son would realize that, no, he would *not* win. There would be a day, I saw right then, when he would be riding his bike in a race set by some older, more adept, probably bigger kid—this Cub Scout, most likely—and he would look up from his own furious pedaling, his holler swallowed down to silence, that smile gone, his eyes losing this joy, and he would see up ahead that the race was already over, that he would lose. He would be immeasurably older that day, so that what I felt standing at that window, my first-born child still riding his bike toward the end of the street, where once again both boys were waiting for him, Zeb still yelling, still oblivious to his loss—was grief.

Grief for the death of my child's childhood, me already mourning the day he would truly lose the race. The race he was in *that* day he did not lose, because he hadn't yet recognized what loss was. Someday soon he would, and that was the day I feared. He would grow up.

What was important about this moment five years ago, I knew even then, was that I had seen into the life of my child, into his joy at simple play, joy that someday would cloud over with the knowledge of loss; knowledge that loss could happen, in fact, even though he rode his bike as fast as he could. Even now, in this moment, today, I can see my four-year-old son's face, hear him hollering, know that he is convinced he can win, even though a Cub Scout on a piecemeal bike whips him every time they race, Zeb not yet knowing what loss really is. And I carry this moment of saddened joy with me, knowing that what really happened was perfect.

And, of course, loss came. It has visited my son on many occasions over the last five years, visited him in the hundreds of small and huge ways loss visits us all. We still live on a cul-de-sac, but now we own the house we live in, a tract home only a few miles from the duplexes. Aaron still lives across the street, our families having decided at the same time that this new subdivision would make a great place to settle.

Zeb wins bicycle races now, but also still loses them. He scores one hundred on spelling tests, but sometimes scores in the fifties in math. Sometimes he beats Aaron at Scrabble, and sometimes he storms into the house from playing with Aaron, angry because Aaron wins at the card games he makes up himself, the rules of which are always evolving, always delivering to

Aaron himself just the right number of diamonds or discard piles he needs in order to win. These card games might as well be a bicycle race with a Cub Scout, I sometimes think.

But the loss I believe brought Zeb into the ranks, that loss I'd been waiting for since that day five years back, came only a couple of months ago. This was Zeb's first karate tournament, an event he'd been waiting for for six months. Winners would be chosen. Trophies given out. He belongs to a studio here in town, goes three times a week to spend an hour or so in his crisp white *ghi* practicing blocks and thrusts and palm-heel jabs and what-have-you. He knows the names for a few dozen moves, can execute them sharp and strong. He's already an orange belt, two belts up from where he started, at white.

This Saturday in spring, as usual, we were late getting out of the house, had to drive the van too fast all the way across town to a middle-school gymnasium already filled with kids in crisp white *ghi*s, parents and grandparents and brothers and sisters and aunts and uncles all crammed into the bleachers. The tournament was for kids from the five different studios that made up the chain. Zeb had signed up for two events, Sparring and *Pinan*. The *pinan* is a series of choreographed moves performed alone before a jury of three adult Masters. Sparring involves two kids with boxing gloves, the two of them kicking and chopping and blocking and doing everything else they've learned in class. This event would also involve, we were pretty certain, pain.

Yet Zeb's instructor, Mr. Mike, a man with a thick south Boston accent and a fifth-degree black belt, assured us after class one evening this event was a no-contact spar; points, in fact, could be taken off if anyone actually hit someone else.

We made it into the gymnasium, quickly lost Zeb to the swirling droves of kids in white *ghi*s, only to hear his age and belt group's sparring match location announced a few minutes later over the loudspeaker. At any given time that day there were six matches going on, areas on the gymnasium floor roped off and assigned, all these children bowing to each other and then doing battle. Around us were parents we recognized from the studio back home, and parents we didn't. But we were all here to cheer on our children, however well or poorly they did.

Even before we made it to the appointed area, Zeb was there, seated on the floor in front of the bleachers in a group of eight or nine kids, all orange belts, all of them his age. Melanie, Jacob, and I made our way up into the bleachers, stepped carefully between parents and siblings and everyone else already seated, all of us smiling and nodding. Since I'd been given a video camera for Father's Day the year before, it was my job to carry it with me wherever we went; my job, too, to record everything. Today was no different, and I tried my best not to bump with the camera the heads of the people we wormed through. Finally we found a few empty seats, Jacob already complaining about being hungry. He'd spotted the hot dog and soda stand in the far corner even before, it seemed, we'd gotten inside the gym.

The referee—I'm not sure of the proper karate name for this person—explained the rules to the children as best he could over the noise of the gym (all these matches going on, all these parents shouting out and cheering): The first kid to be awarded three points would win the round; the match would be a series of elimination rounds leading to a final round, so if you lost a round you were out; you would stay inside the cordoned area, use only accepted karate moves; no contact.

The first few rounds were mild affairs, kids kicking now and again or thrusting huge gloves when they remembered to; mostly they circled each other, wary of doing anything that might get them hurt. This was the case with Zeb's first round, a round he won three points to two. I watched it all through the black-and-white viewfinder of the video camera, saw Zeb make a couple of jabs, a kick or two, only to have the round suddenly finish before me, all of it in miniature. There just hadn't seemed much to see.

I took down the camera then, called out to Zeb. He'd already sat down on the gym floor, and when he turned to his name, I could see this smile on his face, his lips closed tight. He was proud of himself, I knew, but didn't want to let it show too much: There were all these people around, his mom and dad (Jacob had found a friend from school by this time, was up on the top row of the bleachers and messing around) a good five or six rows up and waving, crazy.

Next came a few more rounds to finish out the first elimination, and then it was Zeb's turn again. There he was in the viewfinder, listening to the words the referee gave them both. The two kids bowed, then Zeb took up his stance, danced up and back with the boy, neither landing anything. There were moves, forays and retreats, and then the other boy kicked, was awarded a point. Then the boys went back to the center of the area, started again.

That was when Zeb's belt fell down, dropped around his feet. That was when, too, the other boy kicked again, received another point, Zeb still trying to free his feet from the orange belt there on the mat. The referee quickly picked up the belt, tossed it to the side, and the round went on.

Zeb lost, two to three.

When I brought down the camera this time he wasn't smiling, and when we called his name he turned to us slowly, his mouth a thin line. He only looked at us, puzzled, eyebrows up, eyes open wide. I gave him the thumbs-up sign, and he nodded, turned back to the next round. It was over, just like that.

But then, a few minutes later, it seemed there might be some piece of hope left, some way to salvage this loss: At the end of the second elimination, the referee called Zeb and another boy up for a round. I leaned toward Melanie, said, "What's going on?"

"Maybe they're letting him do another round because his belt fell down," she said, and I nodded; it was reason enough to give my son another chance to win.

The boys listened, bowed, took their stances. A woman two rows down and a few feet over stood, yelled, "Give it to him, Jason. Give it to him!"

Jason, a kid from one of the other studios, gave it to him. His tactic, it became evident immediately, was simply to rush the opponent, thrash him with his fists, hope to land some points in there. The problem was that the opponent happened to be my son, and the boy's move so startled Zeb that he fell backward and landed on the mat, the boy and his arms still working in Zeb's face while the referee pulled him back, knelt to Zeb to see if he was all right. I was watching this on the video camera, all of it over and done with just that fast. And I was startled, too, to see the referee award the boy a point for a jab.

"Good job, Jason!" the woman yelled. "Focus!" she yelled. "Focus!"

I had the camera down now, was watching what would happen in color, big as life. I forgot to turn the camera off, so what happened next, when we watched it at home on video, was all cockeyed and angled, off balance.

The boy focused, focused so well that this time one of his jabs landed squarely on Zeb's jaw, knocked him to the ground.

No contact, was what Mr. Mike had said.

No contact, was what the referee had said.

Melanie stood, then I stood—Zeb on his bottom on the mat, the boy already pulled away again, the ref already kneeling to Zeb. He was crying, I could see, although he nodded at whatever the ref was saying to him. He sat there, his hands in the gloves in his lap, his face red and squinted up, eyes on the mat. The ref held Zeb's jaw with one hand, said more words to him, words lost on the sound in here, lost in the shouts from the woman two rows down—"Good job, Jason," she was saying, "Keep focusing"—and Zeb nodded again. He took in a few quick breaths, brushed at his eyes with the back of a glove.

He was crying, his eyes wet, we could see even from here, as he finally stood, got up and went to the middle of the area, took up his stance again. The referee said a few words to the boy whose mother was cheering him on, but the boy's eyes were wandering, as though he'd heard all this before and didn't really care. It was only a warning from the ref, his eyes seemed to say.

Zeb was gone now, lost the next two points quickly, cowed by the boy with furious arms and a mother to match. When Zeb came back from the round to take his seat on the floor he only glanced at us, his eyebrows knotted up, teeth still clenched.

He'd lost, to a kid who landed a punch instead of played by the rules, just as he'd lost to a Cub Scout on a bike who wanted to race kids half his age. But this time it counted somehow. In the glance up at us in the bleachers I think I saw what was to come: During his next event, the *pinan*, that choreographed dance of self-defense moves he knew so well, moves he performed for us in the family room each night after karate, he forgot himself, stopped dead halfway through, had to start over for the three Masters watching him, and in front of the parents and siblings and everyone else seated in the bleachers watching. He had to start over.

On the way home that afternoon, after all our hugs and words of praise for how well he'd done, and after we let ourselves berate that Jason for the way he fought—berated his mother, too, for putting him up to it—there still seemed to Zeb no comfort, though he nodded again and again at all our words. Even Jacob, all the way in the backseat of the van, joined in now and again. "That kid was mean," he said. "That kid was mean." But Zeb took it all, I knew, for the hollow words they were, the comfortless touch. At a stoplight halfway home I turned in my seat, looked at him. I saw his eyes, the shine in them; saw the way he sat staring out his window, his mouth still that same thin line.

"Zeb," I said, and he looked to me. His hands were folded in his lap. I said, "I'm proud of you." I said, "You didn't give up."

He only looked at me a moment longer, then shrugged, turned to the window again. I glanced at Melanie, there next to me; saw her chin quiver. She'd been the one to stand up first when he'd been hit, and I saw in her eyes the same shine as I'd seen in Zeb's.

"Garrett and me had fun up there on the bleachers," Jacob said. He said, "Can we go to Hardee's for lunch?"

I turned back to the road.

There will be Cub Scouts who want to race you with their bikes everywhere you will ever go, I want both my sons to know. There will be boys who will break the rules just to win fair and square, I want them to know. And still you may lose, I want them to know, too.

Zeb knows this now, though on that day five years ago such an idea was incomprehensible. One thing he *doesn't* know, though, is the gift he gave his father all the way back then, one of the finest gifts he will ever be able to give: the crystalline picture in my head of him on his bike, his hollering, that joyful noise, ringing in my ears, him pedaling and pedaling, the truth of him winning every time.

But the accompanying picture I now have of him, the one of him looking out the van window on a bright spring afternoon, his eyes glistening, hands folded in the lap of his crisp white *ghi*, is no less fine and rare a gift. It's a beautiful gift, different only for the other truth it speaks: He's one of us now, a piece of his innocence broken away, lost as we all lose it.

Atonement

Then there are days like today. We were trying to get out of the house for karate camp this morning, karate camp being a program for kids from eight o'clock to noon for a week at the studio where Zeb has his lessons. Melanie was already gone for work, and the boys, out in the garage, were ready to go. Except for the reefs, those Velcro sandals I'd told Zeb to put on before we ever got outside.

"But Dad," he said, "we're barefoot in the studio. We don't have to wear them."

Then, for all the various and minuscule transgressions that had already been visited upon me this day—when I let the dog out this morning to relieve herself, she made a beeline to the house under construction next door and the discarded chicken bones the framers leave there each day; Zeb and Jake argued, before a single light had been turned on, about who got to use the bathroom first when they woke up; I had to tell Jacob four times to comb his hair; I had to tell Zeb three times to clear the breakfast dishes; the sink was full of pots and pans from the dinner party last night; Melanie was already gone—for all these terrible facts of the day thus far, I blew up at Zeb.

I yelled. I shouted. I threw my hands up in the air, ranted about obeying your father; ranted about the fire ants out there on the grass where we park our old VW Bug, those ants just waiting for bare feet and the opportunity to bite; ranted about never listening to me; ranted about and about and about.

I yelled the first ten minutes of the fifteen-minute drive to the studio, my stomach churned up now about how little writing I'd gotten done the day before, in preparing for the above-mentioned dinner party, about the deadline for a book I'd missed by a month already, about the twenty-two-page story I was about to trash because it had died suddenly the day before yesterday. All of these concerns were translated into a language that involved only words about Velcro sandals, about fire ants, about the idea of obeying your father. My world and its woes boiled down to *Why can't you just listen and obey me without making me yell?*

The last five minutes of the drive we passed in silence, me feeling the stupidity of it all, of my yelling about things that, finally, had very little to do with these two boys. Zeb, next to me, only looked out his window, as did Jacob behind us, the two of them wondering, I imagined, if they dared speak.

But when we parked in front of the studio, Zeb already with his door open, ready to climb out; I reached to him, put my arm around his neck, pulled him to me. I hugged him, said, "I'm sorry I yelled. I shouldn't have done that."

"That's okay," he said into my shoulder.

"Can we go to Wendy's for lunch?" Jacob said from the backseat, sensing this window of opportunity, his father contrite.

Zeb pulled away, smiling, and I turned, looked at Jacob. He was leaning forward, grinning. "Sure," I said. "Wendy's," I said.

Then I looked at Zeb, standing now and pulling forward the seatback to let his brother out. "Zeb," I said, and he looked at me. "You have to wear the reefs so you don't get ant bites. Okay?"

"Okay," he said, and smiled again. By this time Jacob was out. He slammed shut the door, and they turned, ran along the sidewalk to the glass door of the place, disappeared. Just like that.

There are days like today. Days with no story, really, other than the misstep, the idiot words and gestures, the sincere belief for a moment, however blind, that all this yelling might actually do some good, when the world and Velcro sandals seem somehow malevolently aligned against you. Then the right word, the right gesture. The lunch at Wendy's, atonement after confession.

No story, really, other than that of being a father.

First Names

Each morning we heard his small, thin voice above the static hum of the humidifier in his room. "Mommy!" he called.

We had only the one kid then. We lived in Columbus, Ohio, where I'd gotten my first job out of college, teaching remedial English at Ohio State; Melanie worked full-time as a secretary for Ohio Rural Electric.

Getting up, then, was a job in itself. Monday, Wednesday, Friday, and alternating Sundays it was my turn to answer. Those mornings I'd throw back the sheets, slouch to the room across the hall to find Zeb, our twenty-two-month-old, standing in the crib, hair wild, eyes open wide. He stood there, smiling, arms out, waiting for his morning hug. "Mommy! Mommy!" he said.

He was talking to me.

For a long time Zeb knew me as only Mommy, and for just as long I worried over it.

"But I'm his father," I used to say to Melanie, she a few minutes behind me, sometimes still asleep, as she made her way to the bathroom those mornings I pulled first duty, Zeb splayed out on the changing table, his diaper heavy as a bowling ball. She'd rub an eye with the palm of one hand, shake off the night.

"Why not Pop?" I'd say. "Maybe just Dad?"

"It's a blessing," she'd say. "I think it's nice he calls you Mommy."

Sure, he could say Daddy. He usually did, too, those mornings I met with him first. But only after he called me Mommy a half-dozen times, his voice sometimes taking on the squeaky pitch Melanie and I reserved for talk with Baby Bear, his sleep partner. Zeb, newly dusted and with a fresh diaper, would hold the stuffed animal out to me, call, "Mommy! Mommy!" in baby falsetto, just like Mommy and Mommy did each night before turning out the light. Only we'd use his real name: "Zeb!" we'd say. "Baby Bear loves the Zeb!"

So why not Daddy first thing?

He wasn't slow, never had been. Not by a long shot. I remember one afternoon Melanie and I were in his bedroom, folding clothes and putting them in the cardboard dresser, one of those put-together kits we'd found at Kmart—this was straight out of college, remember, when it seemed miracle enough that we even owned a real-live crib. We were discussing plans for worst-case scenario Potty Learning measures. Zeb thought, as far as we could tell, that his training pants were some strange form of socks, happy with them only once he'd gotten them down around his ankles.

In the midst of our words about what actions we might take

if he hadn't been housebroken by middle school, we heard water running in the bathroom.

Drowned, we thought as we ran from the room, *or scalded.*

We found him only standing on the toilet, the bathroom cup, filled with cold water, in his hand. He turned off the faucet, took a drink from the cup, then dumped what was left in the sink. He put the cup down, leaned across the sink, pulled his dinosaur toothbrush from his dinosaur-toothbrush holder, and looked up at us. "Toot paste?" he said.

He wasn't slow. Not at all.

Melanie thought his calling me Mommy was nice. But what if it had been the other way around? What if he'd called *her* Daddy? I didn't dare form the question in real words, though; I knew I'd get an answer quickly, one that would cut: *You didn't give birth to him!* she'd have shouted. *You didn't cry when he was weaned!*

But I was there in the delivery room, I would have countered. *I coached you, I calmed you, I soothed you. I fed you ice chips.*

You told the doctor to turn the mirror the other way so you couldn't see what was going on down there! she'd have shot back. *You told him you might throw up!*

True. She would have me on that one. *But I burped him after you fed him,* I would've feebly put in, the argument already lost. *I rocked him to sleep nights.*

You didn't leak through your shirts, she would have said.

Argument over: She would have won. And his calling me Mommy first thing in the morning still would have been a blessing.

———

He had other words, too, that he made to mean other things. He knew his mother and I were two different people; it was *I* who had the problem. One afternoon, for instance, we were on our way from the apartment to pick up Mommy from work, and we stopped at a drive-thru teller to make a withdrawal. When I pulled away from the window, Zeb said something, a one-syllable word.

"What?" I said, and looked in the rearview mirror to get a good view of him in the backseat, strapped like some pre-Mercury monkey into his car seat.

"Fries?" he questioned. "Fries?"

I looked away, ashamed, and felt his innocent brown eyes piercing the back of my skull, his word an accusation: More than once I'd been guilty of stopping at the Wendy's drive-thru window on the way to Mommy's office, squandering our hard-earned pay on fries and a Frosty. Of course I'd had to share them both with him each time, too, to keep him from squealing on me.

"Sorry," I said. "No fries. That was the bank." I held up the twenty-dollar bill, waved it at him back there. "See? Money."

"Money?" he said.

His first request.

There was, too, the language he'd learned just from being in the car with me all those times. When he heard a car honk, whether out on the road or on TV, he shouted, "Hey, *bud*dy!" drawing the *bud* out loud and long, though whenever I shouted it to the clod going eighteen miles an hour in front of me, I didn't give the phrase quite that inflection. Whenever the car stopped, too, whether in traffic or as we pulled into our parking space at the apartment, he hollered, "Cowboy!" This was a contracted form of my own "Come on, cowboy," a generic term I used on any given driver who forgot to signal or who stopped to let cars go ahead and turn left in front of us. I used to wonder, too, what he would think a cowboy really *was* once he got older. What would happen when his friends called for a game of cowboys-and-Indians? Would he climb into the nearest car?

I made the mistake once of talking about this problem of first names in the morning to one of my colleagues in the remedial English department. She was an intellectual—I knew she was one by her coffee mug with the logo and call letters of the local public radio station printed on it. She suggested this problem of mistaken names might have something to do with what she called Primary Words.

"Primary words," she said, "are words that mean many things. Words like—," and she went quiet. She thought. She brought the coffee mug to her lips, took a sip, as though the mug itself might give her the words she meant. She put the mug down, finally said, "Words like, like, *cleave*. Cleave. Cleave, you see? *Cleave* is a primary word."

I'm still not sure what she was saying, but I nodded, smiled. This was my first job, and I wanted to be an intellectual, too. She was, in addition, the mother of a twenty-month-old, and I knew that if I pressed her for an explanation, asked her what she meant, she might've shouted, *You didn't leak through your shirts!*

I guess, though, that I knew all along it was all my fault, his turning *Mommy* into a generic term. It's a hazard of the new way of parenting, the splitting of lives as evenly as possible right down the middle, even to the point of making certain neither of us prepared four dinner meals two weeks in a row. We took turns cleaning the house, took turns grocery shopping, even took turns washing the car. And we changed diapers, fed him, washed him just this way as well. So why *shouldn't* he have called me Mommy?

I even remember sweating back then over the whole How-old-is-your-baby question. "Twenty-two months," I'd answer when asked. I know *my* father would have had to stumble, try to piece together a good answer: "Geez, two?" I can hear him say. "A little less than that? Something." It wasn't that he didn't love me. It's just that, well, things are different now.

For a long time, too, believe it or not, I struggled with the dilemma of what to call him two weeks before or after a month-birthday. What would I say when he was twenty-two-and-a-half months old? Go for broke, say twenty-three? Some ironclad formula seemed in order, though none ever came. And when would I stop counting months?

"How old's your boy now?" I could see someone asking me.

"Oh, he's a hundred and eighty-six months," I'd have to answer. "Taking him down for his learner's permit next week."

He's nine now—109 months, to be exact—and the days of his calling me Mommy are long gone. The sad thing, though, is that I can't recall the first day he called me Daddy when I went into his room. I could make up a story about it, here and now: I could tell you how it was a Tuesday—Melanie's morning—

and how there seemed something different in his voice as I came up from sleep, the sheets on Melanie's side of the bed already thrown back, my wife slowly rounding the footboard on her way out of the room. I could tell you I closed my eyes then, pulled the sheet up a little closer to my chin, and a moment later she came back into the room, her feet still dragging across the carpet, while my son still called out from his room. The sound of his voice *was* changed, I could tell you, different somehow as it made its way out his room and across the hall and into my ears, and I could tell you how I felt then the give of the mattress as Melanie climbed back into bed, me turning to her, asking, "What's wrong? This is your day," my eyes still closed.

"Guess again," she would say. "Listen."

Then I could tell you of that word coming to me, his small, thin voice calling out above the static hum of the humidifier in his room: "Daddy!"

The truth is, though, that I can't say any of that happened at all, though I'm certain there had to be a first morning. And now that he's 109 months old, it's not even Daddy much anymore. Just Dad.

But I think I see the blessing that first name was, what Melanie tried to tell me those mornings she was yawning and getting to go to the bathroom first, and maybe what Zeb was trying to teach me, too, all along: It wasn't a word but a person. The one who took care, picked him up, held him. The one who mattered to him.

Melanie. Me. Either one. Both.

Learning Sex

"Boys pupate at around age fifteen," Zeb said, very matter-of-fact, and climbed out of the van, pulled his backpack from the seat. We were in the garage, just home from picking the boys up at school. Jacob, as always, was the first one out, already gone on his bike, roaming the neighborhood on his daily after-school route.

"What?" Melanie said, already out of the van. She glanced at me, then back to Zeb. She was smiling, and pushed closed her door.

I was at the top of the steps up from the garage, the keys out for the door. "They what?" I said, and turned to him. I was smiling, too. Already I could see Zeb's face going red at our reaction, these words and smiles regarding his scientific assertion.

"Pupate," he said. "Your voice changes. You get hair." He paused. "A lady from the Medical University talked to our class today." He slipped the bag onto his shoulder. He wouldn't look at us. It was then I remembered that a little over a month ago he'd come home and told us about metamorphosis in butterflies, the whole business of spinning cocoons, worms turned into miraculous flying creatures.

That was when, too, I laughed, and I wonder if I'll be held responsible years from now for some complex Zeb will have, traced to me and that laugh: I see a woman, his wife, yelling at me about their sex life, about her husband's penchant for laughter in the middle of things.

Melanie cut her eyes at me, signal enough to stop, though I could see she was holding back laughter of her own.

I took a breath, said, "You mean *puberty*. They go through *puberty*."

He looked up at me, smiling himself. He shrugged, said, "Yeah. That's it."

I put the key to the door, unlocked it, opened it up. " 'Pupate,' " I said, "that's good."

"Actually," Melanie said from behind me, and I heard her start up the steps, "that's a pretty good idea of what happens."

"I told you it was true," Zeb said.

True.

Boys pupate, revealing, once it's all over, bigger boys whose voices have changed, who have to shave, who need deodorant and mouthwash and Odor-Eaters for their tennis shoes. And make ready for girls who have recently pupated, revealing themselves to be young women.

Learning about sex, of course, figures in here.

Right now Zeb, at age ten, knows more about sex than I did at his age. I am certain of this, as Melanie and I took it upon ourselves last year to have The Talk with him. We decided the summer before he started fourth grade that we wanted to tell him the truth of where babies came from, how they were made—our decision a result of the ugly mutant facts Melanie and I were given around his age, what has always been referred to as "picking it up on the street." But I can't help but think his pointing at hula dancers on the television set one evening while we were watching a *National Geographic Explorer* episode, then his two-word assessment of what he saw—"That's sex"— pushed us to the brink.

We got out our copy of *Reader's Digest ABC's of the Human Body*, one of those all-in-one reference manuals you get for three easy installments when you send in your sweepstakes tickets, and set out to set Zeb straight. It's a good book, a helpful one with all the right cross-sectional diagrams and photos, from the chart of the male reproductive system that looks for all the world like a sad map of Florida, to the diagram of the female reproductive system, the names of items in there like a list of planets in a parallel solar system: *ovary, uterus, cervix, vagina, clitoris, vulva.* Here, too, is the photograph of sperm, hundreds of lost dogs wagging their way toward a home they've never been to before, and the white pinpoint that is the egg itself, in this particular photo "approaching the feathery edges of the Fallopian tube."

We told Jake he could watch TV in Mom and Dad's bedroom, a treat unknown to the boys, one that would assure our privacy in the kitchen. Then we brought Zeb in, had him sit at one of the three chairs we'd pulled out from the kitchen table. "There's some things we want you to know about before you start school this fall," Melanie started in.

Zeb crossed his arms, looked at the two of us with the level stare he employs when he thinks he's in for trouble: head slightly bowed forward, eyes half closed, lower jaw jutting forward. His look.

"Do you know where babies come from?" Melanie went on, smiling.

"Yes," he said, too quick. He held his arms tighter, let out a quick breath. "I know," he said.

"Where?" I said, and he looked at me. I knew my word had come too abruptly, simply there and aimed at him. I knew he didn't know. So I smiled, tried hard with that smile to soften what had sounded like a cross-examination.

He shrugged.

"We just want to tell you," Melanie said, and leaned toward him, "so that when somebody at school tries to tell you something crazy you'll already know the truth."

He looked at her, his arms held even tighter now, his lower jaw jutting out hard.

Melanie still smiled. "This way you'll already know the truth," she said again.

Then, slowly, she turned to me. "Bret?" she said, and smiled. "Go ahead."

I looked at her. I took a breath, swallowed. I said, "Oh," then turned to Zeb.

He was looking at me, his eyes thin slits. Then he put his hands up to his ears, covered them.

I remember looking at my mom one night at dinner and asking flat out, "Where do babies come from?" This must have been back around fourth grade, as best I can recall. Right about the time I *picked it up on the street*. But I remember asking that question in all sincerity, and I remember, too, my dad's instantaneous reaction, enough to make me flinch: "Hey!" he shouted, and I quickly turned to him, saw him leaned toward me, a fork in one hand, a knife in the other, his forehead knotted up, his eyes right on me. "Hey," he said again, "don't talk like that!"

I am not kidding. That's what he said.

"Bill," my mom said, and I turned, saw her looking at him. She was smiling at him, her head slightly tilted, lips together, the corners just turned up. This was her What-is-your-problem? smile, and I knew she was on my side. "He just asked," she said. I turned back to Dad, waiting to see what he would say.

His eyes flicked from mine to hers to mine to hers. He sat up straight in his chair. By this time all four children were looking at him, waiting. He said, "Well," then put his fork and knife to the pork chop on his plate. "Well," he said again, "this isn't the time or the place. It's rude."

That was it. And even though Mom was on my side, I still didn't get an answer.

I know, though, that I must have asked this question in the fourth grade, because that was when Danny Kortenburg and George Ross showed me where babies come from. They thought, of course, I was an idiot for not knowing, as though they'd been born with this superior knowledge, had owned it all their lives. The two of them, there in the boys' bathroom at Larkspur Elementary School, decided to inform me, this retard, how it was done.

"I can't believe you don't know," Danny Kortenburg said, and pushed his glasses up on his nose. "Just like dogs," George

Ross said. He had pale blond hair, freckles, what my dad called a snaggle tooth. Danny Kortenburg was about a foot taller, his brown hair buzzed off on the sides, a lock off the top always falling down into his eyes. "You're on the bottom," he said to George, who turned to him, said, "No way, you're on the bottom." The conversation went on this way for the next few minutes, precious recess time lost while the secret of the universe was being kept from me by two boys bickering over dogs and who was on top.

Finally, Danny pulled George's arm behind his back, said, "You're on bottom," and George, his face twisted up in preadolescent anger at being one-upped by this bigger kid, said, "Okay."

Then George bent over, put his hands on his knees. Danny jumped onto his back, sort of hopped up and down like he was riding a horse. "This is what your parents do," Danny said, and now both he and George were laughing. "Uh-uh-uh," Danny said, and George straightened up, Danny falling backward and onto the green tile of the bathroom floor.

I stood there, my arms crossed, leaning against the sink. I said, "No way." I said, "You guys are stupid. No way," and started feeling sick to my stomach, imagining my parents doing this weird acrobatic feat; and I wondered, too, who was supposed to be on top, wondered if parents fought over that just like these two guys were doing.

George's face went serious, and he put his hands on his hips. Danny, still on the floor, pushed the lock of hair up from his forehead, touched his glasses. Slowly George nodded, then whispered, "Yes way." It was in this manner I picked it up on the street.

I wouldn't get The Talk, though, the straight news about sex, for another four years, until I was in eighth grade. I do not now recall what events precipitated my parents' decision to tell me the facts on this particular evening, though I know I didn't point at hula dancers on TV, make pronouncements regarding copulation. By the time I was in eighth grade I and some friends— Mark Beck, Steve Noeding, Jim Loeffler, and Chris Penney, to name a few—had built a fort out in the desert between our tract and the junior high. Where our tract ended, on Thunderbird Road, the desert began; two miles away lay Greenway Junior High; halfway across was a beat-up and discarded couch, two folding chairs, a fire pit, all of it settled beneath a palo verde tree and surrounded by tumbleweeds. Our fort.

There, for what now seems years, we stared at and joked about and huddled around and passed back and forth the same creased and crumpled pages torn out of somebody's dad's issue of *Playboy*, a blond there with breasts impossibly large, a smile so alluring it seemed to speak to each of us newly each time we pulled the pages from where we'd stashed them in the springs beneath the couch. So when my mom said to me one evening, "You and your father need to have a talk," and when my dad looked at her, then at me, swallowed, blinked, and said, "All right, let's go," and headed off down the hall back toward their bedroom, I was already familiar with the terrain of the female body, knew so very much about sex and what it entailed. There'd been some fine-tuning here and there regarding that horseback stuff since fourth grade, and now I wondered precisely what it was my dad would have to say.

I followed him into their bedroom, the same room in which I'd imagined them *not* playing piggyback. He stopped at the foot of the bed, turned, pointed at the valet next to the dresser, a small piece of furniture that had a low seat and high back, the top of which was shaped like a hanger, for Dad's suit coats.

I sat down, the seat so close to the ground I had to look up at him as he sat on the bed, facing me. His eyes hadn't yet met mine. He had on a dress shirt and slacks, no tie. He put his hands on the tops of his thighs, lifted them, let them drop, then moved them back and forth.

"Well," he said.

He said, "Okay."

I had him, had him in a way I'd never known before: my dad, powerless, stunned. So, to make matters worse for him, I said, "Go ahead. I'm listening."

He looked at me, finally, his hands still. "Well," he said, and looked back to his hands. "What do you want to know?"

I shrugged, let the question hang in the air a few moments before I said, "I already know."

"Okay," he said, and breathed out. "Good. That's good." Then he laughed. It was a good laugh, a solid laugh, a kind of laugh I hadn't heard or seen before: It was a laugh that didn't take me into account, didn't pretend to cajole me or to praise me. He wasn't even looking at me. This was just laughter.

His hands started moving again. He shook his head, all without looking at me. "Well, then, is there anything *you* want to tell *me?*" he said. And he laughed.

"Sure, Dad," I said, me an eighth grader given courage, suddenly, in the wake of my dad's revealed weakness. "It has to do with girls," I said.

He stood, laughed again, and then I stood, once more the follower, having lost in this single action, simply standing, whatever power I'd had over the situation, and over my father.

We started back down the hall, toward the kitchen. My mother stood at the counter, waiting, arms crossed. "That was fast," she said.

I said, "He asked me for advice." Dad laughed once more. He was looking at Mom now, and I could see in the way he looked at her, his eyes open wide, eyebrows up, there was relief there, this momentous occasion in the childhood of his second-born over.

That was my The Talk, the one everyone either gets or doesn't. I got one, but got one that gave me nothing. Only a glimpse of my dad without armor, defenseless, stunned. I liked it.

Of course no one learns sex except through experience, and even then one finds its true meaning, or meaninglessness, only when the act is woven through with love, or stripped of it. Images on a creased and crumpled page from a magazine, vague imitations in a boy's rest room, a father's stunned silence, even actual forays once we believe we are *in love* mean, finally, nothing.

Zeb surrendered his hands from his ears once we brought out the diagrams and the photos, his eyes wide open and taking in the images there. I don't remember what I said to start things off, nor what Melanie said, either, only know the words were blessed enough to line up in a semblance of factual order, Zeb finally laughing at the notion that this tiny *sperm* from the dad's penis actually broke into this tiny *egg* that had settled inside the mom's uterus to make a new and real live human that grew until it was big enough to live on its own, until it became a baby that—this was where he seemed most jovially impressed—actually was squeezed and was pushed from inside the mother through her vagina to become a living, breathing person.

He laughed, though it wasn't nervous laughter, I knew. Relief, I believe it to have been. Sort of like what my dad gave out to me: laughter of relief about this whole huge mystery: *sex.*

But we finished off this astonishing set of facts by revealing to him the greater truth behind it all: that this is all a result of love for another, of respect, of care. We told him, as we believe, that this is all a part of what it means to be a *husband,* and the woman with whom he would someday have sex his *wife.* Sex was and is and will be a sacred act, a gift from God, carried out after love has been secured through marriage, inside that sacred vow before God.

Zeb nodded, smiled.

Now he knows the truth. Boys pupate. True. We find out about sex one way or another. At least—and at best—both Zeb's mom and dad have had a hand in how he came to find out.

The mystery of it is still revealing itself to me, here in my own marriage: The truth is that Melanie is more beautiful now than when we were married; our private life, the schematic we outlined for him with charts and diagrams and strange names, only grows more fulfilling, more rewarding the longer we know each other.

We were in the van and backing down the driveway early one evening a week or so ago, Melanie beside me, the boys in the backseat, headed out for dinner at the local Mexican restaurant, a place where the boys practice their elementary Spanish on the waiters, all of them fresh from Mexico.

"Wait," Melanie said, "my sunglasses." I stopped the van there on the driveway, and she climbed out, crossed in front of us, headed up the walk for the front door. She had on a sleeveless cotton blouse, a denim skirt, huarache sandals; and there was something in how her hair fell as she looked down into her purse for her keys, and something about the sun on her shoulders, something about the back of her neck, that made me say out loud, "She's beautiful, isn't she?"

The boys were quiet behind me, watching, I imagined, their mom. Finally Zeb said, "Yeah."

She made it to the front steps, started up.

Then came Jake's voice: "Hubba hubba," he said. I turned around, looked at him. He was looking at me, grinning. "Ooh, baby," he said.

"Where'd you hear that?" I said, and tried to keep from laughing.

"Garrett," Jake said, still grinning. "He says that all the time about Sarah and Elizabeth." I only shook my head, faced forward, waiting now for Melanie. One down, one to go.

Jacob

"How you doing?" I say over my shoulder, and see my breath, a white veil, hang in the air.

"Fine," Jacob says from behind me; then, "Faster." He is four, his birthday only two weeks ago.

We are out on the street, a dozen or so houses down from ours, me with my hands at my back pulling the rope tied to the inner tube Jacob is lying on. We've been outside most of the day, and now the sun has already slipped behind the thin line of trees to my left, the pines above the houses black now, silhouetted in the dusk of a winter evening. My bare hands and face sting with the cold, my lungs charged and sharp with the air in and out. Still I walk on, move faster across the thin glaze of ice on the street.

This is Christmas Eve, 1989, the houses heaped with snow, the lawns and driveways and sidewalks all blanketed. Only the street is visible, the thinnest layer of brand-new ice the only proof of what work the sun has done all day to melt this white.

Just yesterday the sky was the old slate gray we'd grown to recognize as a snow sky when we lived up in Massachusetts, a flat and even gray that signaled what was to come.

It came, gave us ten inches of snow the day before Christmas Eve, then cleared early this morning to reveal this day, a day filled with snow angels and makeshift cardboard sleds and trying to dig out with heavy garden shovels. Nobody has any snow shovels. No sleds. I couldn't even find my gloves. This isn't Massachusetts. It's Charleston, South Carolina; there hasn't been a white Christmas in fifty years, the news anchors and the papers have all trumpeted. Ten inches of snow in one day and one night.

"Faster," Jacob says again.

But I stop instead. We are headed away from our house, even though I can feel the temperature dropping, the sky growing dark. A few people on the street have already turned on their Christmas lights: white electric candles in the two-story to my right, alternating greens and reds lining the roof on the house to my left. We are headed away simply because Jacob asked me to tow him. I look up, see the sky directly above us, a blue so crisp and close and certain it seems I might be able to reach up, burn my fingers on the cold of it. I wait for Jacob to say something, to protest or urge me on or, simply, ask why we've stopped.

I turn, look down at him. He is lying back on the inner tube, his legs over the end closest to me, his mittened hands out to either side. We found the mittens still clipped to the sleeves of the hooded gray snow jacket he has on, a leftover from when Zeb was his age and we lived in Ohio. His head is back, the hood drawn down tight around his face: red cheeks and nose and chin, mouth, eyes. He has on sneakers, two pairs of my sweat socks over them. We couldn't find Zeb's old snow boots.

He is looking at the sky, too, at that blue, and suddenly I see the color of the snow banked on the sidewalks and in the yards and on the roofs, see everything, even the glazed asphalt and that inner tube and the gray hooded snow jacket, even his face; I see all of it giving up to this blue, a shade so sharp and cold and beautiful I have no choice in that moment but to look up at the sky again, this time to see what my son might see in it, this brand-new four-year-old on the first white Christmas Eve in fifty years in this town we live in. I want to see what he sees.

It is a blue sky, of course. Nothing more. But *blue*, a blue growing darker each moment we stare up at it. I look back at him again, watch him a few moments. He is moving his mouth now, letting out small breaths that shimmer in this blue air, then hang right there above him.

I say, "Are you cold?"

He stops moving his mouth a moment, then says, "No."

"You want to go home?"

He is quiet a few moments longer, seems to weigh the implications here, though he is only four: no more rides on the inner tube, no breaths you can see. No more blue. He says, "No."

We are getting dinner ready, me with the ribs out on the barbecue, Melanie with the salad and rice in the kitchen. Zeb is in the kitchen, too, setting the table, pouring milk. We've had forty-one days in a row of temperatures over ninety degrees; dinner most nights is a matter of salads and something cooked outside in order to keep the kitchen from heating up.

We haven't seen Jacob in a while, not since he was sent upstairs to take a quick shower a good half hour ago. Upstairs has been strangely quiet, no sounds of water running, as far as either of us can recall, and so I have pictures of him either sprawled out on his bed and reading—he's only seven, and already halfway through the Boxcar Children series, Henry, Jessie, Violet, and Benny Alden living in him every day—or sprawled out in the playroom, watching TV without permission: a bad habit of late. I head upstairs, see the boys' bathroom door is closed, the light on in there, and I knock, open it up.

Here is Jacob, face down in the filled tub. His head shoots up then, and he turns, looks at me. He has on his swimming goggles, the yellow plastic ovals half filled with water. He smiles—grins, actually: *I bet I've been in here too long*, that grin says.

In the tub, too, are at least fifty various toys, everything from a squirt gun to a Daffy Duck figurine to dinosaur stick-ups you wet and throw against the wall, where they stick. The toys are in the water, littered about the front of the tub, back behind the toilet, some even in the bathroom sink, and I feel then the wet of the bath mat I'm standing on: He's tracked in and out of the tub, I know, retrieving toys, testing them, evaluating them.

This is his tub time, after all; here's this grin, those goggles, his bare white butt there in the water, the deep, rich tan of his back and legs that much darker for that white butt. But I sent him up for a quick shower, the ribs done and growing cold right now on the kitchen table. So I say, "Finish up. We're about to eat."

"Okay," he says, still grinning; only in the grin is a minute change, a fraction of a facial muscle somehow moved into a different meaning: *I got away with all this,* that grin says. Then he turns, plunges his head with those goggles back into the water.

Because he knows he got away with it, I try for a moment to play a joke on him there in the water, think to do something small and funny but just a little bit ornery, just to let him know I know he knows he got away with something. The bathroom has no windows, and I put my hand to the light switch, just to be a little ornery, and I turn it off, the room black now.

I expect him to give a startled sound, say, *Turn that back on!* or, *What are you doing?* I hear him pop up from the water again, imagine him looking around. I wait for him to react, maybe even chew me out a little for scaring him so.

But he only says, "Wait a minute, wait a minute," very matter-of-fact, and I hear him turning in the water, moving. I flip the light back on. He's sitting in the water now, his hands to the opposite end of the tub, down by his feet, those hands moving in the water there. He's still got the goggles on.

He says, "There's a glow-in-the-dark shark in here somewhere." He lifts a hand, holds up to me a pale green plastic shark six inches long. "See?" he says, grinning.

I have no choice then but to take the shark from his hand, hold it up to the light above the mirror a minute or so, then toss it back into the tub. I turn out the light, close the door behind me, and we two stare at the shark there under the water, a bright green wavering with the movement of the water. "See?" he says again.

In one day we've driven from Salt Lake City to Gunnison, Colorado, with a side trip to Arches National Park. Roughly seven hundred miles altogether. We rented a car in Dallas a week and a half ago, have been making a circuit that started there and led through Amarillo (friends), Ulysses, Kansas (an aunt and uncle), Denver and Cheyenne and Laramie and Rock Springs and on down to Salt Lake (grandparents). Now here we are, high on the plains in the Rockies.

Jacob is only three and a half, can barely see out his window, Zeb having just turned six a couple of months before. He can't see much more out his window, either, and so the two have been left largely to look at each other all this while, and at the books we've brought, the baseball card packs or Matchbox cars or crackers and cheese we've meted out every hundred miles or so. We've stopped along the way, taken in as many scenic overlooks as possible. And, miraculously enough, even after twenty-six hundred miles and a week and a half, they haven't yet asked *When will we get there?* But the last few miles down toward Blue Mesa Reservoir and Gunnison were twisty, and we had to stop once to let Zeb throw up. We've all been in the car too long.

The motel we've checked into is a few miles past Gunnison proper, a town with a single intersection, though a big one, rows of storefronts north and south, east and west. The Gunnison Lodge sits beyond all this, due east of town, all alone on the high prairie here. It's an imitation German chalet, the two-story building sided with dark wood and rough stone and green Bavarian-style picket fences; the lobby sits inside an A-frame. Our room is on the first floor, and out our window we can see mountains a few miles away, on the other side of the highway.

No forest here, only bare rock, dry grass, this highway, above it all an empty late-afternoon sky.

After we unloaded, we found our way to the Jacuzzi room, where we sat for a half hour or so, careful not to let Jacob stay in there too long at a stretch, the water so warm. Now we are here in the motel restaurant, a German place: the walls the same wood and stone, the carpet a deep red, the furniture heavy and dark.

We eat, eat like we haven't eaten in weeks, though in Moab we stopped at the Tastee-Freez on the main strip, ordered burgers and onion rings and shakes. The beans and spaetzle and sauerbraten and veal and everything else we eat here is wonderful, the restaurant, Melanie and I marvel, a real find out here in the middle of nowhere.

Zeb eats, though not too much: He's still feeling a little strange after the incident in the car. Jacob sits in his chair, his chin barely reaching the tabletop; they have, for some unknown reason, no booster seats for kids, and he sits there feeding himself spaetzle and spaetzle. By the time we finish it's dark outside. We didn't start dinner until well past eight-thirty, the sun already down by then, the sky above us as we crossed the parking lot from our end of the motel to the restaurant—right off the lobby and under that A-frame—still blue, still light.

But now it's dark, and as we emerge from under the A-frame and go back out into the lot, I look up, see the stars. Tons of them, spread across the sky, a surprise after a day spent beneath a white and baking sun, a surprise after seven hundred miles across blacktop, beside us rock, above us wide open and empty sky.

A surprise, one so strong and strange and welcome I stop,

there in the lot, and only stare, try to take it all in. "Whoa," Zeb says, and I look at him, see him standing beside me on my right, next to him Melanie, and I can see in the dark out here the two of them looking up, too, astounded.

"It's beautiful," Melanie says. I look back up, afraid I might miss something, but then I feel something at my left leg, and I look down, see Jacob clutching my leg, looking up at me. Not at the stars.

"No," he says. "I want to go back," he says.

I reach down, take his hand. I say, "Look at the stars. Look at how many of them there are."

"No," he says again, and now he looks down from me, presses his face to my pants, shakes his head. "I want to go back."

"He's afraid of stars," Zeb says, and gives out a laugh. Easy for Zeb to laugh, I think, settled there between Mom and Dad in the middle of a restaurant parking lot, more stars above him and his brother than either have ever seen before.

It comes to me: It was light when we came in, dark when we left. We're in an unknown place, what might as well be a different planet, for all Jake can tell, and now what are these things above us, these bits of light in a huge black sky, a sky bigger than any sky he's ever seen before?

"Come on," I say, and I squat, take him up in my arms, lift him up to settle on my hip, the way his mom did with him when he was so much smaller than he is this day. He looks at me a moment, then looks up at these stars, his hands clasped at his chest, and leans into me. "They're stars," I say. I say, "It's okay. They're beautiful."

Still he leans into me, still he looks up at them, still his hands are clasped at his chest. Then he puts a hand out, points to the sky with his index finger, the others all curled into a three-year-old's fist. It lasts only a moment, this assertion of himself into the multitude, and then his hand is back to his chest, and he leans his head into my neck, settles there. I can't tell if his eyes are open or not.

But here has been his hand, out in the dark, pointed at these stars.

Slowly we move across the parking lot, and I look at that sky filled with stars, feel the weight that is no weight in my arms: Jacob.

Melanie and I are on the sofa in the family room, watching the six o'clock news. Behind us sit the boys, at the table in the kitchen, the two of them working on cherry Popsicles. We haven't yet had dinner; the Popsicles are because two weeks ago Jacob had his tonsils out, and we promised him as many as he wanted for the two weeks after the operation. Zeb, of course, has one because his brother has one.

Jacob, at age five—three more weeks and he's out of Montessori preschool for the summer, kindergarten at a public elementary school looming before him this fall—has had on average ten to twelve ear infections a year since he was born; he's had tubes put in his ears twice, the first time after it was revealed through hearing tests that he had only 30 percent of his hearing in both ears, his speech way behind. Hence, finally, the tonsillectomy. The operation went well; he was home that afternoon—surgery that when we were kids was a weeklong affair, now relegated to an outpatient procedure.

But yesterday we got a call from the preschool to let us know it seemed he was bleeding a little. Melanie and I went down there, picked him up. He had a little blood at the corners of his mouth; his tongue was red as well. As soon as we got home, we called the doctor, who told us to meet him at the emergency room.

There we watched him peer down Jacob's throat. "Looks like the scabs are coming off," he said, then flicked off the little light, turned to us. "This is normal," he said. He smiled, shrugged. "Believe me," he said, "if there's a problem, you'll know about it." I looked at Melanie, who looked at me. Zeb was busy unwrapping a depressor he'd found in the drawer. Jacob only sat on the gurney, hands together in his lap, his legs off the edge, mouth closed.

We looked back at the doctor. I said, "What do you mean? What could happen?"

He shrugged again, nodded. "You'll know if there's a problem. Believe me." He put the light into his front shirt pocket. "But this is normal." He looked back at Jacob, put a hand to his shoulder. "You're fine, sport," he said.

Now Jacob coughs behind me, and I turn, look at him there at the kitchen table. "You okay?" I say, and he nods, the Popsicle jammed in his mouth. I turn back to the TV, and he coughs again. And again. It's a short hack, nothing long or clouded. Just a quick, hard cough.

"I don't want any more of this," he says, and both Melanie and I turn, see him with the dripping Popsicle held out from him, red juice slipping down his fingers to the vinyl tablecloth.

"Just finish it up," I say. "You pestered us for it, you couldn't wait until after dinner. Now finish it."

We turn back to the TV; I hear another two coughs, then his voice: "I can't finish it."

I turn once more. They've both been eating three or four Popsicles a day for the last two weeks, and I've come to believe they're just taking advantage of us, living the age-old dream of Popsicles ad nauseam. Jacob's fine, I think: Just last night, after the episode at the emergency room, we went to our neighbors' across the street for a cookout, where Jacob had two hot dogs, potato chips, and root beer, then played Frisbee on into dark, the Day-Glo orange saucer a weird shard of flying color in the backyard evening light.

"Look," I say, "you have to finish it. You asked for it, you finish it." I turn back to the news, hear yet one more hard cough, then the tough scrape of a chair across the floor, quick movement, and the sound from the powder room in the hall of Jacob vomiting.

We are up in an instant, Melanie and I, and make it to the bathroom a moment later, the two of us jammed in the doorway to see our son hunched over the toilet, the toilet filled with a crimson so thick and bright I know, certainly, it's not Popsicle juice but blood. Drops of blood are spattered on the wall beside the toilet and on the toilet seat. I crouch down next to him, see bloody spittle trailing out his mouth, him breathing in and in, and I see, too, how pale his ears have gone, his cheeks—and he vomits again: more blood.

"This is it," I say, too loud, my voice banging through the tiny room. "This is what he said," I say, and mean the doctor, what he told us we would know.

I call the doctor, who says to meet us at surgery. "Just go right through emergency and to surgery. They'll be ready for you," he says, cool and calm, and hangs up. Melanie is still in the bathroom with Jacob, who is crying now, howling, and I see Zeb standing in the bathroom doorway, watching.

"Let's go," I call, "let's go. They're waiting for us," I call, and for some reason I grab from the dish rack on the counter the clear plastic Tupperware container we use to keep ground coffee in. Without the lid, I think, this will be useful if he throws up again.

Melanie is crying now, says, "Jacob, oh, Jacob," and walks slowly out of the bathroom with our son, Zeb backing away, and I see the spittle down Jacob's chin. In that moment Melanie reaches back into the powder room, grabs the hand towel on the ring in there, and wipes his mouth. His face is too pale, his hair, it seems, darker for the loss of color to his face.

"Carry him," Melanie says to me, and I realize I am only standing, looking at him, an empty coffee container in my hand. I stoop to him, gather him up, a five-year-old who seems to weigh nothing to me, and I start down the hallway to the front door, where Zeb already stands, the door open.

Jacob coughs again, that same cough, and again; and I have only enough time to set him down on the landing at the bottom of the stairs, hold the coffee container under his chin before he vomits yet again.

He fills the container with blood, and I am thinking, *I do not believe this is happening.* He loses color even as he sits before me, crying into the container, blood dripping from his open mouth, his arms going pale, and his legs, his fingers. He doesn't even open his eyes, merely slumps down on the landing, and I hand up the container to Melanie, who disappears into the powder room, flushes the blood down with the rest he has lost, and reappears.

I pick him up again, my son now limp in my arms, and run to the van, where Zeb, this wonderful other son of ours, has opened the van door, and waits. Melanie climbs into the passenger side, and I hand her Jacob, who settles into her lap still just as limp but even more pale now, a pale I have never seen before, of course, because I have never known anyone to have lost this much blood when I was around; and I close the door, urge Zeb into the backseat, then come around to my side, start it up, back us down the driveway, and to the hospital.

Traffic is thin, no lights we have to run, and we make it there in seven minutes. I pull up, drop Melanie and Jacob off at the sliding doors, which open at the presence of our van, then pull around to park.

Zeb holds my hand as we hurry through the white rooms of emergency, faces turning to us and nodding, no smiles: They know who we are, where we're headed; then we're to the wallpapered halls of the hospital proper, on our way back to surgery. We were here just two weeks ago, I'm thinking, here in this small community hospital, where a tonsillectomy is a simple procedure, nothing to fuss over, and now I reach with my free hand to the heavy wooden door to surgery prep, open it, and see across the small nurses' station Melanie standing at a gurney in another room, in front of her and out of my line of sight my son: I see only the bunched sheet around his legs.

I get to the room still with Zeb's hand in mine. There lies my younger son. Jacob's not asleep, I can tell; his head moves back and forth, slowly, as if under water, and his eyelids lift open now and again, barely, to reveal his eyes rolled back, only the whites visible. The anesthetist is there in her blue scrubs, asking what he's eaten today, while a nurse inserts an IV in the top of his hand, and now the doctor enters, nods at us, still cool, calm. "We're taking him in right now," he says; then, "Don't you worry."

The words, of course, are empty ones, as hollow, I hear, as that simple diagnosis yesterday—*This is normal*—and as hollow, too, as his cryptic warning: *You'll know if there's a problem.* As idiotic, I finally hear, as the veiled threat exerted by a father tired of his children pestering him about Popsicles: *You asked for it, you finish it.* Now here we are.

"The throat has hemorrhaged," the doctor says. "We'll have him patched up right away," he says.

But I am only looking at Jacob, his eyes rolled back, the whites there; and now I see, too, how white his lips have become, white and cracked in only these few minutes, and I see his eyelids, too, are white, now nearly transparent, his face white and growing whiter, and then he is gone, wheeled from us, Zeb still holding my hand, Melanie following after the gurney a step or two, all the nurses quiet and moving away from us.

The old moment has come to us for the second time: Melanie's been having contractions since two-thirty this morning, and now it's five o'clock, the contractions three minutes apart. Today is December 10, 1985, a day exactly two weeks after the due date; later this morning we were to have gone in to the hospital to have Melanie put on Pitocin to bring about labor. It came anyway.

Her mother is here in Columbus. Tired, finally, of waiting to get the call to come help us, she flew in from New Jersey three days ago, and now, at five A.M. and dressed in her flannel nightgown, sees us groggily to the door.

Outside it's still pitch black and now strangely warm; we had snow a few days before, and then came a warm front, melting it all. The streets are wet, no ice, a thin fog above the empty streets. "I'm going to run a few red lights," I say as we head for the first intersection, "just like on TV. If the police stop me I can say, 'My wife's having a baby!' " Melanie laughs, puts her hand to the dash, swallows down that laugh.

But we get no red lights, only greens the whole way from Westerville to Riverside Methodist. "Shoot!" I say each time one turns green, just to be funny. But Melanie isn't laughing anymore.

By ten that morning there's been no change: just these contractions, time and again, each about the same length, the same intensity; until, finally, an intern comes in, gently inserts a long metal rod that looks like a darning needle into Melanie to burst the amniotic sac.

It works, and by eleven-thirty the doctor, a woman we have never met before, is there and guiding her, Melanie's hand in mine and squeezing down hard, my free hand with ice chips, my mouth with words that, it seems, don't do much other than sit for a moment in the room, then disappear with the next series of preordained breaths: six *hee*s and a *whoooo*.

Then, at 12:05 P.M., he's here, a baby wet with blood and fluids and howling as the doctor hands him to me, the boy already in a white towel; and he's warm, this thing is *warm*, and he's crying, and now I'm crying and I move from the foot of the bed to Melanie, now with her arms up to me and to this new child in the family, Jacob Daynes Lott, howling away, the sound of his voice piercing and beautiful at once.

But I come back to this day before Christmas, when snow has come to a place it hasn't come in fifty years, like some late but supreme birthday present to a boy who's just turned four.

Six months before this moment stands a summer night high in the Rockies, a year and a half later stands an afternoon of Popsicles and more blood than it seemed was involved in the birth of both my boys. Three and a half years later stands a moment in another bathroom, this one with the light off, a glow-in-the-dark shark in the bathwater our mutual focal point, while four years and two weeks before this early evening and inner tube and sweat socks over sneakers stands the beginning of it all: a crying baby, the warmth of it.

Each of these contributes to what this whole thing, *father-hood*, means. Even my hollering out to Jake about the need to finish a Popsicle once started, the stupidity of that remark still a year and a half from this moment in the cold.

And even in this moment, the sky and all things around us growing blue, Jacob lying back on the inner tube and staring up at the sky about to let stars seep through, there stands just another twenty minutes or so ahead another moment revealing yet more stupidity of a father: Jacob and I will, twenty minutes hence, march into the house from our excursion through the neighborhood in the dusk of Christmas Eve, and Melanie will size us up, then take note of how Jacob is shivering, his lips pale blue, he is so cold. *Stupidity,* I will think: *How I could I be so stupid as to not bring him home sooner than this?*

But even as she will quickly take off his jacket and pants and those socks there in our foyer, the same foyer from which we will rush to the hospital a year and a half later, Jacob will smile up at me and say to his mother, "We went for a walk. Daddy towed me."

All this, I believe, is what fatherhood is about: stupidity, adventure, threats, silence, blood, fear. The immensity of a night sky. Love.

All this lies before us, and behind us. For now, though, there is only this moment, the two of us on a street glazed with ice, the world growing blue.

Hugo

For a year, beginning with those days before we had power restored, Jacob drew pictures. He was three years and ten months old when Hugo hit, and even now, four years later, with Hurricane Emily bearing down on the eastern seaboard, Jacob's eyes dart too fast, his questions come just as quick: "Will we go away again? Is the hurricane going to come here? Do we have to get water? Is the hurricane going to come here?"

He asks on our way to the Texaco station off 17 Bypass this afternoon, where we're headed to fill up the propane tank for the gas grill, just in case. Zeb's in the backseat of the Bug, holding the tank upright with one hand, in the other a Tom Swift paperback. Jacob's in the seat next to me. We've already made one trip to the Harris Teeter, stocked up on canned goods, paper plates and towels, peanut butter and powdered milk and all else that won't spoil, just in case. Melanie's taken the van to Wal-Mart for batteries and an extra flashlight, just in case.

Jacob asks questions all the way to the station, looking out his open window at me, back at Zeb: *How many flashlights*

*do we have? Can I have one in my room? Do we stay home from
school?*

Two. Maybe. No.

We pull into the station, and I see the line for propane: ten
or twelve, most with one tank, a couple here and there with two.
I've been getting the tank filled here for the last four years and
have never waited in line before. Even from where I park on the
shoulder just beyond the outside island, I see, too, the red face
and sweated-through shirt of the attendant, a huge kid with no
neck working the nozzle from the great white tank surrounded
by a chain-link fence. He probably hasn't worked this hard at
the station, ever.

"You guys wait here," I say, and open my door, pull back
the seat.

Zeb tips the tank toward me. He hasn't been asking any
questions, comfortable, I figure, with the prospect of a hurricane
coming. He's been through it before, too. I pull the tank out,
close my door. "This is going to take a few minutes, so don't
you guys start fighting out here, okay?"

"Yes sir," Zeb says.

"Okay," Jacob says.

I cross in front of the Bug, start for the line of people snaking off toward the tank.

"Dad," Jacob calls from behind me, and I turn, see him
looking at me out his open window. I can see him from the nose
up, the seats so low in the Bug. His eyebrows are knotted, eyes
open wide.

"Yep?" I say, seeing in only his eyes, his forehead, that he
is afraid.

He is quiet a moment, then says, "We'll wait for you in here."

"Okay," I say, and smile, wave, try to act as though I'm not afraid, too.

The pictures he drew: Four years ago, in the months after Hugo, Jacob filled entire tablets of drawing paper with page after page after page of black scribbles. The crayon in his hand, he sat quietly at the kitchen table or on the floor of his bedroom or, once the flooded preschool had been put back in order, at the drawing table there, and scribbled.

The lines run up and down, fill the page.

There are hundreds of them. We saved them, like some sort of dark talisman against what might happen again, though we've told him for the last four years that Hurricane Hugo will never come back, there will never be another Hurricane Hugo. Which is true: That name will never be used again.

Still, here comes Emily, last year Andrew, so that this truth is not true—a hurricane can slam us any day it so chooses—yet we still comfort him with the fact no Hugo will ever return.

He peeled off the first picture from his Snoopy drawing pad in the kitchen the third day after we'd come back home from the evacuation. He held out the piece of paper to me and without taking his eyes off the drawing said, "That's Hurricane Hugo."

There are hundreds of them.

———

Our story is a pedestrian one, and might seem in the face of other stories broadcast from down here even mild: We left home Thursday morning at eight, drove the prescribed back-road evacuation route all the way to Columbia, a hundred miles north, where we climbed on the interstate, headed another hundred miles west to Spartanburg and friends we'd called the night before, had asked if we might stay a night or two.

Until the emergency broadcast system took over the television Wednesday night, the night before Hugo hit, that ugly loud tone blaring out of the set, no mention of this being "only a test" after it, we'd thought all this was an adventure of sorts: the batteries, the canned goods, the flashlights and topping off the tank in the car all exercises designed to make us feel in control of the situation.

We stayed up that night, slowly packed into the van what we believed we needed, those priceless items: two boxes of photographs, another box filled with baby books and artwork and mementos, the file of "Important Papers" that included the mortgage and birth certificates and savings bonds and all else deemed Important, the two disks my novel-in-progress was on, the silver, my set of five original bobbing-head Beatles statuettes (I have two George Harrisons). Next had come the gas grill, still in the box. We'd bought it only that morning at Brendles; we'd talked about a gas grill for a while, and now seemed as good a time as any. Next came clothes for a few days, the cooler, books for the kids to read, pillows, stuffed animals. All of it stashed into the Caravan some time after midnight.

Then we dutifully taped big Xs on all the windows. Somebody'd told us that was the thing to do to save your windows from a hurricane: tape Xs on them. I remember doing our bedroom last, the double-panel windows there nearly impossible to reach. I had to lean out the frame, turn around, and put the tape on the outer panes, all from the second floor.

But there was a moment when, after I'd finished the last window, I stopped, looked out onto the backyard. All the lights were on downstairs, casting long squares of light out across the lawn, back toward the huge pines at the end of the lot.

"Melanie," I said, "come look at this."

She leaned out the window beside me, the two of us jammed into the frame, and we got down on our knees, leaned as far out as we could, looked at the dark out there and these squares of light below us. The wind was up, shifting through the pine boughs, whispering, and we only listened, no words between us. We could see stars up above the pines, and I remember wondering if all this were for nothing. We could see stars out here!

Then I heard Melanie crying beside me, the sound of her breathing the same soft whisper as the wind through the boughs. I only put my arm around her. We'd be okay. It was headed for Charleston, after all. Here we were in Mount Pleasant, a good six miles to the north. We'd be okay.

The boys were asleep.

The next morning we had some breakfast, the van already loaded, then climbed in, backed down the driveway, headed for Spartanburg. But once we made it to the street, Melanie said, "Stop. Stop."

"What?" I said, and put my foot on the brake.

She climbed out, and I saw she had the camera in her hand.

She walked down the curb until she was even with the middle of our yard, then stopped, brought the camera from its case, took a picture of the house. When she turned, headed back toward us still parked there in the street, she wasn't smiling.

She climbed back in, said, "The 'Before' picture." She tried to give a smile.

"The before what?" Zeb said from behind us.

"Before what?" Jacob said.

I looked at Melanie, then at the boys. "Well," I said, "just in case something happens to the house from the hurricane, we want a picture of the way it looked before the hurricane came." I tried to smile, too.

"Oh," Zeb said, and gave a quick nod, then looked out his window, squinted his eyes at the overcast sky. Jacob looked at Zeb, then at me, then out his window. He said nothing.

We made it to Deno and Kathy's five hours later, unpacked the clothes and sleeping bags, and spent the rest of the afternoon and evening and night watching television.

Zeb and Jake played with Deno and Kathy's children. Dylan was a year older than Jake, Haley a year older than Zeb, and although I am certain our boys were aware of something going on at home—every time they came in the house for something to drink, they saw us glued to the television—they gave no evidence the hurricane was on their minds. They were playing, as children should be allowed to do when matters are out of their hands and when the children themselves are out of harm's way.

That night the hurricane hit, and for some reason the only reports we kept getting on Deno and Kathy's local stations were from Myrtle Beach, a good ninety miles or so to the north of Charleston, clearly out of the path Hugo was predicted to take. We stayed up late, watched *Nightline* and all they were reporting, including the wreck of an airplane at the end of a runway at La Guardia; and I remember resenting somehow this intrusion, the way suddenly an airplane in New York could upstage the wrath of a huge hurricane, a single man-made machine taking over the airwaves when it was my house down there in Charleston at stake.

When we finally went to bed it was well past two, the boys in their sleeping bags on the floor of Haley's room, the room where we would all sleep, the only room they could spare. It was a little girl's room, New Kids on the Block posters and pink-striped wallpaper and fuzzy stuffed animals. The bed where Melanie and I were to sleep was a single, covered with a circus clown spread.

We lay next to each other and turned, dreamed, lay awake, believed for a moment we might have slept, only to turn over, realize we were awake again, the two of us jammed into the bed, our boys on the floor, sleeping away, tired and happy at the long day of play behind them.

But sometime that night I awoke, saw in the moonlight through the blinds that Melanie was, finally, asleep. I could hear my children breathing in the dark; heard Melanie, too; but above the soft whisper of their breathing I heard something else, a rush of sound, sharp and solid but still almost too quiet to hear.

I stood from the bed, stepped over Zeb, who lay between the bed and the door, then went out into the dark hallway of a friend's house, a place I'd never stayed before, an alien place designed, at least for this night, to give shelter to us strangers from two hundred miles away, and I wondered what at that precise moment was going on at my house.

I went down the hall to the living room, that room where we'd parked for hours watching the set; then turned, went to the door that let out onto their carport and the backyard where all our children had played that afternoon. Still I could hear the sound, that rush.

I opened the door, not certain what I would find, and the sound suddenly increased, now loud in all its quietness, a whisper shouted. I looked up, past the eaves of the carport roof, and saw that same moon, the one Melanie and I had stared up at only the night before, when I'd believed six miles from Charleston might be enough room to let the storm pass, my wife silently crying beside me as though this were the end of the world as we knew it.

Here was the sound: Just beneath that moon were the tops of the pines in their yard, huge pines at least a hundred feet tall, and the wind out here—there'd been no wind all day long, simply an overcast sky—charged through the boughs, bent the pines side to side in big, slow arcs, the air through needles whistling furiously, and I wondered why no one else was up, no one else out here, startled from sleep by this sound. There were no clouds, only that moon, and these trees, and that wind.

Two days later we made it back; we'd had to wait a day while road crews cleared the interstate, I-26, choked with knocked-down trees. We left Spartanburg at lunchtime Saturday, all our cargo in tow, as well as a roll of tar paper, a gallon of tar, some nails, a cheap hammer. On Friday we'd finally gotten through to a neighbor three doors down, Lisa Meadows, Melanie's best friend and the wife of a Mount Pleasant police sergeant—the reason they had to stay—who told Melanie that in fact our house didn't look too bad. Part of the roof had been stripped bare, she'd said, a window broken out, some siding torn off. Tar paper and nails, some tar seemed about all we needed, I figured.

Splintered-off and uprooted trees, pine and live oak alike, started appearing a good sixty miles from Charleston. I slowed down at the first one we saw, a raw, broken tree pushed just off the highway, there on the shoulder, all four of us looking out the window as though this were a bad car wreck. Then came another, and another, until slowing down for each seemed stupid: This was the way things were along I-26 now.

We made it to Charleston at dusk, saw everywhere what we would realize in the days that followed was routine devastation: roofs gone, trees down, windows broken, the absence of light spread across it all like some invisible blanket, nowhere any electricity, so that as we made our way across the Cooper River bridges and down to Mount Pleasant, one whole side of the Ramada Inn at the foot of the bridge torn away to reveal rooms with pictures on the walls, furniture, wall lamps, the motel a life-size dollhouse here in our hometown, that lack of light made this all even more surreal, unbelievable, as now we passed the roofless transmission shop, the fire station with one whole wall stripped away, intersections with no traffic lights and little or no traffic, broken trees on the median, in the street, in parking lots, and on houses.

When finally we made it to Six Mile Road and the right turn off 17 back toward our tract, the sky behind us was a dark yellow, all light almost gone, our headlights cutting the way before us. Yet even in that growing dark we could see gray light through the open doors of the middle school's gymnasium there at the corner of 17 and Six: The entire roof of the gym was gone, above it only the twilit sky, filling the room.

The boys, behind us in the dark of the van, said nothing. Six Mile is only a two-lane road, and here, two days after the hurricane, the road crews clearing fallen trees hadn't yet arrived. I drove slowly along the road, weaving around and between the trunks and branches on the asphalt, beside us darkened houses and shacks; then we were at Rifle Range Road, and I turned right, weaved through more trees, our development only a quarter mile ahead.

Here we were. Trees lay across the road, in front yards, through and in homes; roofs were stripped to the plywood, walls stripped to the insulation. Debris lay everywhere: asphalt shingles, boards, vast lengths of siding, branches, gutters off roofs. All this in only the light from our headlights.

And, finally, here was our house: 2032 Presidio Drive, our driveway littered with shingles and needles and branches. We pulled in, headlights on the garage door and the window beside it, X-ed with masking tape. I left the lights on a moment longer, looked at Melanie.

"Here we go," she said.

"Go where?" Jacob said from behind us, on his voice an edge: fear, I could tell.

"Just into the house," I said, and tried to make my voice sound strong, though I was afraid, too, afraid of what we'd find inside, in the backyard, everywhere. Afraid of what this place would look like in daylight.

"We're just going to go take a look inside. Don't worry," I said, then shut off the lights, the engine, and opened the door, climbed out, the flashlight from the grocery sack between the front seats already in my hand.

We headed for the front door, me first, then Melanie, then the boys, and as I turned the key in the lock I heard Jacob say from behind us, "Hurricane Hugo did this?"

"Yes," I heard Melanie say, and then the door was open. I shone the flashlight through the foyer, saw nothing out of the ordinary, then went through the front hall to the kitchen, where things looked fine as well, my family trailing behind me.

"Slow down," Melanie said, and Zeb and Jacob said at once, "Slow down."

I made it to the kitchen window, shone the flashlight out onto the backyard, and saw our two biggest pines down back there, the same trees we'd listened to only Wednesday night. The trees seemed to fill the lawn back there, cover everything, and I only stared at the mass of bark and splintered wood and green branches. Melanie was beside me, and took in a breath. "Oh no," she said, and now here were the boys beside us as well, looking out into the dark.

"What's that?" Zeb said.

"Trees," I said.

Jacob said nothing.

We went next to the stairway, still not certain what to expect of all this. So far things seemed in order; the broken window Lisa'd told us of was only the outer pane of a double-paned window in the living room; the siding had been stripped from the house to no more or less an extent than anyone else's, judging by what we'd seen of the stuff on the road as we'd driven in. So far the house seemed fine, given it had been through a hurricane.

I looked up the stairs with the flashlight, started up, Melanie and the boys following. We looked first in the boys' room, found nothing, only their bunk beds, their toy boxes, stuffed animals all waiting as though nothing had happened. Then we went farther down the hall, the light from the flashlight corraled by the walls so that behind us was pure black, before us bright white, shining on the linen closet at the far end.

"No," Jacob said. "I don't want to go."

I was at the end of the hall then and turned, shone the light toward him. "We're just looking. It's okay."

"It's okay," Melanie said, and took his hand. He held on to hers with both his.

"I don't want to go," he said, but by that time I'd already turned, was headed into the study. There on the floor lay two feet of attic insulation, the blown stuff. At first I didn't know what it was, only saw this loose brown material, what looked like mattress stuffing, piled up against the wall, there between the filing cabinet and the closet door, and across my desk, the book-shelves, everywhere. I had no idea what it was, or where it had come from; and then I turned the flashlight to the wall, saw a gap in it where the ceiling and wall met, a gap big enough to fit my fist into, and saw, too, the gap where two walls met in the corner of the room: The Sheetrock had separated, torn loose somehow from ceiling to floor and halfway across the room.

This was attic insulation, I saw only then, the stuff having shot through this crack in the wall from the attic above us. I went to the wall, put my hands to it.

It moved, swayed out from me, the gap growing larger, the

entire wall separated from the house from attic to foundation. This was an outside wall, eight inches from my fingertips the night outside, and I saw for an instant a wall falling down, collapsing to reveal this room and the master bedroom next to it, just like the wall at the Ramada Inn.

"All right," I said, "everybody out. Let's go to the Meadows'," afraid in that moment, and for the next three weeks, before we got a structural engineer out to look at it, that the wall might simply peel away from the house.

Jacob was the first one down the stairs.

The story past this point is one of recovery, of adapting, of patience and impatience, and of a four-year-old boy doing his best at it all by scribbling with a black crayon; his older brother oblivious, it would seem, happy just to be standing on the trunk of one of the pines out back, or sailing a shingle like a Frisbee through the yard—what Zeb did most days, waiting like all the rest of us for the world to set itself back in line.

In daylight the house was worse than we'd been led to believe, the crown vent that ran the entire peak of the roof ripped off, leaving a six-inch hole from one end of the attic to the other. Rain from the hurricane and this next new storm, a cold rain that'd arrived overnight, simply poured into the attic; the heat pump had been lifted from its mounting and torn from the house, lay now on its side in the grass of the backyard; water had shot in between the windows and sashes, ruined the carpet everywhere, and had somehow gotten into the computer, ruining that as well; the soffets, those pieces of siding mounted beneath the eaves, had all been blown out, leaving bare studs in places;

a good third of the siding was gone, and those stray pieces still left on the houses were bent, crooked; nail heads had popped through the Sheetrock in the house, the force of the house's buckling enough to separate one whole wall of the house; enough, too, to make those nails poke out.

The new tar paper stretched over about two-thirds of the hole left by the crown vent.

Later that first morning back, in what we believed would be some act of redemption, of triumph over this catastrophe, another neighbor, Dave Gaines, and I set about in that cold rain to remove the live oak that'd crashed through the garage of the widow's house across the street. We had only two axes, the tree itself a good six feet around; still, it took us three hours of chopping before we realized the impossibility of the task, so stunned were we at what had happened to our world. For those three hours we truly believed we could take apart this tree, and by extension truly believed we could set the world in order, if we only tried. We could not, and surrendered, finally, exhausted, broken, there settling in us for the first time a piece of reality: We could do nothing here.

But eventually four of us, armed only with hammers, a few pounds of nails, and an extension ladder one of us owned, started roaming the streets of the neighborhood with the good intention of patching people's roofs with the shingles that littered the ground. We finished off my house, then moved on to Steve and Lisa's—Steve still on duty, still on duty—then to Tom's, and to Dave's and Carla's, and to Bruce's, next door to the widow's, and it seemed then that only by banding together could we get something done: roofs patched, the rain temporarily kept from pouring into attics already sodden with the water from the hurricane. But it felt like we were doing something.

Much as it must have felt when, on the third day, Jacob found in the cookie tin we used for crayons that black one, found the Snoopy tablet, and found in a moment of discovery as pure and real and terrible as my touching a wall, then turning from it to hurry my family from the wall I thought might fall away from us at any moment, that he was doing something, finding a way to hold on to what had happened, wrestle it, make it his own, no matter if it would take him hundreds of times before, finally, he believed he had gotten it right, and in getting it right, could let it go.

It took me five hours to put that gas grill together, and we cooked everything on it, from canned soup to steaks to, one morning, at the boys' request, Pop-Tarts, roasted right there on the grill; Melanie and I slept on an air mattress in the dining room for two weeks, the boys in sleeping bags in the living room, us all afraid that wall would fall down; we read at night by Coleman lantern, cooked community meals with all the neighbors, made ice runs to the Piggly Wiggly when we heard on the radio the trucks had arrived.

And Jacob drew Hurricane Hugo.

We had no power for twelve days; the reason we finally got it back, our subdivision bumped up on the priority list, was because the sewers were beginning to back up into the houses, the pump station on our line having been shut down all that while.

The morning it came back on I was home alone. Zeb was

back at Jennie Moore Elementary and his trailer classroom there, its roof peeled back at one corner to let sunlight or rain fall into the room, whatever the weather on a given day. Jacob was back at the Montessori preschool he attended, the mark three feet up the walls where the water had hit not to be painted over for a few weeks yet. Melanie was on a road trip to Myrtle Beach to make a presentation for her architectural firm. She'd left early, stopping first at the office in an old house downtown, where they had power already, and where she could get a hot shower.

I could see through the woods behind our house the electric company's trucks, see the flashing yellow lights, though the pump station was about a half mile away. Twelve days before, it would have been impossible to see those trucks, the woods so thick. But now out beyond the back of our lot there stood a forest of broken trees, too many to count, the absence of trees letting down to us too much light, the skyline changed forever. They'd all been snapped off about five feet up the trunks and lay discarded now, lost.

Then the kitchen light came on.

I turned on every light in the house, turned on the TV and hiked it up loud, ran the dishwasher and the clothes washer, even turned on the empty oven, then set about vacuuming the entire house, elated now at invention, at civilization, at *electricity*. Once I was done with that I went outside and mowed the lawn, watching out for the roofing nails that shot out of the mower now and again, and which would for the next year or so, all as a way of setting the world in order now that power had returned: I wanted even the lawn to be sharp.

It was sunny that day, a warm October afternoon, and when

I'd finished with the lawn I stood at the curb looking at the trimmed grass, at the porch light on and the driveway lamp on, the garage light on as well. Here we were, on the road to recovery. But then I took in the roof once again, the bare plywood up there. And the siding, that broken window, those gutters gone.

I looked down the street, saw where a thick wire from one of the poles lay on the pavement. Sparks flew from it. I went back into the house, called the power company, the adrenaline flow in me already waning: We had a long way to go.

We would not be finished with repairs to the house until the middle of January, the total bill $30,000 on a $95,000 house. And we were lucky: We know people to this day who are still wrangling contractors and insurance companies, see even today houses with tar paper on the roof, no shingles. The trees are still gone, those two huge pines that sang to us on the eve of catastrophe only ghosts now.

But one evening in mid-December, a full three months after the hurricane hit, our older son, Zeb, the boy over whom we did not worry, the boy who we believed had miraculously passed through whatever stresses this disaster had had on our family and home simply by playing outside, Melanie and I preoccupied with Jacob's drawings and drawings and drawings, presented us with a book he'd written.

We still have this, too, eight pages of computer paper bound at one narrow end with sixteen staples all in a row, the date at the top—12/18/89—then, in yellow marker, the title:

A SHOTING
STAR CAME
DOWN TO ERTH

Beneath it, in dark blue ink,

BY ZEB LOTT

At the top left corner, just beside the row of staples, is a star falling down, behind it a trail of yellow slashes signaling its descent.

We were in the kitchen making dinner, and here was Zeb, holding the book out to me. He was smiling, satisfied at what he'd done in secret. Once I'd taken the book from him, he stood with his hands on his hips, waiting. I read it out loud.

"Chapter one. One day there was a meteor shower and a meteor struck the earth. Ca-bowy!" These words were in pink ink, on the middle of the page a jagged figure of some sort—a *mytyer*, as he'd written it—hitting the ground.

I turned the page. "The next day on the ground there was bricks all over the yard," I read: this still in pink, more jagged shapes on the line that represented the yard.

"Chapter two. The earthquake," I read, though his rendering—*erthqwaq*—gave me a little trouble. "One day there was an earthquake." Here he'd drawn a building with eight windows, quivering lines on either side of it to show it was shaking. There'd been an earthquake in San Francisco, of course, on top of our hurricane. One more item for the agenda.

"No one could stop the earthquake," the next page read,

and here stood a stick man with a frown, beside his head a word balloon, inside it, "I quit."

Of course what this was all about was lost on neither me nor Mel as I read it. She stood next to me, had looked at the pages as I'd read them, and now I looked at her, saw her mouth in a tight smile, her eyes going from the page to me to Zeb and to the page. Even only five pages in, we could see that certainly this all had had an effect on him as well. How could it not have? It'd taken three months for it to find an exit.

I looked at him, smiled, said, "This is great."

"Keep going," he said, hands still on his hips, eyes half closed now, as though he'd already won some war of his own against a world that had been shattered by mytyers and erthqwaqs.

I turned the page. *Chapter 3 the Stars*, he'd written, then, *at last the erthqwaq Stopd! and in the sky the stars weare wihte*. I didn't read this out loud, the words, his hope and deliverance, too sharp in me. Beneath the words was a row of blue stars of varying sizes, clear and clean there against the white of the page.

I turned to the next page: *and the raste of the nite it was come*. Now the stars were all the same size, closer together, perfect. I looked at him, then to the page, and read out loud, "And the rest of the night it was calm."

That was when Melanie knelt to him, held him, said, "That's beautiful, Zeb," and I saw him close his eyes altogether when she hugged him, saw his arms move to hold her. Still he smiled. In this manner, Zebulun was delivered from Hurricane Hugo. There were no more books about disasters after that one, no drawings. Nothing. Only a boy pleased and content with the work of his own hands, this book.

Jacob's last Hurricane Hugo was one he made a year later, in his kindergarten art period. He took a sheet of black construction paper, pasted on it a hundred or so small construction-paper crescents of all colors, the pieces settled into a funnel shape against the black, the chaos of those crescents given order in his design.

He brought it home, handed it from his book bag to me. I looked at it, said, "This is great"; then, "What is it?"

He looked at me, incredulous, his mouth open, eyebrows up, as though any idiot could tell. "Hurricane Hugo!" he said, on his voice no edge of fear, not even a trace. Rather, it seemed there was some sort of reprimand implied: *Of course it's Hurricane Hugo.* We framed it, and it hangs now on my office wall.

There is more to this story, of course: the first night "home" spent on the floor of Steve and Lisa's, us afraid of sleeping in the house before we got a better look at the wall; and the barrels of food we ate that night, all that thawed meat; the bald, jovial insurance agent from Ohio who came out to the house, wrote us up in an hour, had our money to us the first week of November; the contractor, Harlon, and the homemade tattoos he had in the flesh between thumb and forefinger on either hand, scratched in the left, JENNIE, in the right, MATTIE, the names of his two daughters; the low drone of gas-powered generators all night long at those households that could afford them, our windows open for the heat and lack of air-conditioning; the care packages, Ellie and Bob up in Massachusetts sending down from Zabar's dried fruit and nuts and crackers and cheese, Chris and Elizabeth up in Vermont sending down pancake mix and pure maple syrup; the four hours, two rolls of paper towels, gallon of gasoline, and six razor blades it took to remove, finally, those big masking-tape Xs.

And the "After" picture, taken that first morning we were back: bare plywood, stripped siding, yard littered with debris, the tree wall behind the house only a thin veil.

Now, four years later, Emily heading our way, that treeline is still pretty much the same; will be, the Forest Service says, for another fifty years. And as I stand in line with the others at the Texaco station, all of us passing our time waiting for propane by telling war stories of how we battled Hugo—the man in front of me, with two tanks, had his house float off the foundation— I think once again of those drawings, Jacob's own battle scars, scores of them; and of Zeb's book, an allegory delivering the world from its own terrors.

I wonder, too, what they think right now, the two of them in that red VW Bug parked just past the outside island. They are watching me, I can see. Me, their father. If only they knew how little I know, how helpless I feel in the face of what could come. A tank of propane, some canned soup, an extra flashlight: my own vague scribblings with a black crayon.

Then Jacob waves to me, as though he can see I need this from him. Then Zeb, from the backseat, gives a smaller wave, an affirmation of some kind, it seems, and I turn back to the line, pick up the tank, and move it forward a foot or so.

Wadmalow

An October Sunday, and I've been in front of the television dangerously long: It's halftime in the second game of a football doubleheader, and at this moment I cannot name any of the four teams to which I've surrendered the afternoon.

Like some thick drab blanket thrown over the day, the sky outside hangs low, rain on and off and on again, so that there was no clear plan for any of us once home from church. I'd wanted to work out in the garden some, try and weed around the tomatoes and crookneck squash and yellow-meat watermelon, maybe even mow the lawn; the boys had wanted to practice headers and goalie kicks out back, too.

But there's that sky, and the two of them—Zeb, age nine, and Jake, age six—can only take a few minutes of the football game before they grow antsy, both with an eye out for any break in the clouds, any letup in the rain. Each time they get out in the yard, kick the soccer ball around, the soft rain starts up again—what Jacob calls a *sprizzle;* part sprinkle, part drizzle—

and here come the two of them again, both boys tumbling back inside the door from the patio, their wet and grassy sneakers leaving tracks through the family room and into the kitchen, where they both stop, pull open the refrigerator, stare inside as though new food might have miraculously found its way in there since last they looked, maybe ten minutes before.

Now here's Melanie, my wife, hands on her hips and, it's easy to see, tired of us all: me in my video stupor and sprawled on the sofa, strewn about me empty soda cans and bags of chips; the boys, wet and bored, wanting only to find food and something to do.

"Why don't you go for a drive?" she says, and suddenly the day seems salvageable, and with her words I see the football game for what it really is: one long beer commercial broken up now and again by glimpses of men banging heads together; and now the sky outside seems somehow not so much a force, either. When I'm driving, whether day or night, rain or shine, I'm in command of the road, in command of our destination, in command of *the day*. She knows, of course, how much I like to go for drives.

But the boys don't think this such a good idea, and both give out heavy sighs, twist their faces into cartoon configurations to show how awful an idea this one is.

"Oh Mom," Zeb says, and lets the refrigerator door close.

"Oh Mom," Jake says, always his brother's echo in such crises as these.

"And take the dog, too," Melanie says. At this, Willa, our black Lab asleep on the family room floor, cracks open an eye, wary of what it might mean that her name has been mentioned.

By this time I'm already up, the notion of simply driving enough to shake off the torpor that lying prone for hours on end, eyes to the set, can give me; and when I take the keys from the key hook by the coffeemaker the dog is up, too, the sound of keys at any given moment her signal: We're going somewhere. She likes drives just as much as I do.

But the boys still aren't convinced. "It's rainy," Zeb says. "It's boring," Jake says.

"I'll stop at the Circle K for snacks," I say. And we are off, the boys nearly beating the dog out to the van, where the sprizzle has stopped for the moment.

"Where are we going?" Zeb calls from the far backseat. We are spread through the van, Zeb in the far back, Jake in the middle row, me at the helm, Willa riding shotgun. Separating the boys is a precautionary measure, as hands have a way of not keeping to themselves, inevitably leading to a slow slide into trouble. Willa, of course, believes herself in charge of us all, her ears perked up, eyes on the road as though sizing up the distance between our van and the Impala in front of us, gauging as best she can the car lengths and my speed in order to calculate proper braking distance.

"I don't know," I say, and glance back in the rearview mirror, where I see Zeb looking out the window to his left, Jake out the window to his right.

"You said the Circle K," Jacob puts in, and looks at me in the mirror.

"Fine," I say, "but after that, I figure Wadmalaw Island. Rockville."

"What island?" Zeb says, though he doesn't turn from his window.

"Wadmalaw," I say, and smile at him. "The onions?"

"Wadmalaw Sweets," Zeb says, and I can see the smallest smile on his face. Zeb loves onions, would eat them like apples if we let him.

"You said Circle K," Jacob says again, and I see him, eyebrows furious, a look on his face of perceived betrayal, as though I'd gotten him into the van under false pretenses: Instead of orange soda and M&M's he's getting an onion.

"Don't worry," I say. "We'll stop." Already we're on the old bridge over the Cooper River, behind us Mount Pleasant and home, above us that same drab blanket of a sky, beneath us the cold and sharp gray-green river.

Before us lies the Charleston Peninsula itself, a thin spit of land paved with rooftops and church spires and wharves and freight cars and more church spires. Then, a few moments later, we're heading down and off the bridge into wet Sunday-afternoon traffic on the crosstown, the rain still stopped though the windshield wipers are on for the mist thrown up by the Cherokees and Peterbilts and Miatas in front of us as we all wind along 17 South, this upper part of the peninsula choked with fast-food restaurants and Medical University outbuildings and parking lots and more fast-food restaurants.

Then it's over the Ashley River Bridge, a short, squat cousin to the bridge over the Cooper, and in to West Ashley, suburb to Charleston and still just as choked as the crosstown, the highway here lined with tire stores and drive-thru banks and Piggly Wigglys and $1.50 theaters.

Amazingly there's been no word from the seats behind me, and I glance up at the rearview mirror, afraid for a moment of whatever wordless mischief in which those two back there might be engaged.

But they're asleep, both of them, mouths open, heads lolled back, eyes peacefully closed. I turn off the radio then, turn right, and leave 17 once we've made it over the James Island Bridge and the Inland Waterway. No sailboats are out this day wanting the drawbridge up, and it seems only a few minutes since we were home and mired in television and wet sneakers. I ease onto Maybank Highway, the state road that leads back to Wadmalaw, look at Willa, still alert in the seat next to me, still watching, and I say quietly, "What did you want at the Circle K?"

She turns to me, licks her chops once or twice, then it's back to the road and her vigil.

I'm careful now not to find potholes, dips in the road, my boys asleep in the car on a gray Sunday afternoon.

Slowly, slowly, the reason why I love this drive becomes evident: As we make our way across James Island, the homes and stores and gas station mini-marts and all other shining proof of man's hands seem to fade until, once we've made it past the last holes of the Charleston Municipal Golf Course—the links empty and soaked, the sky still not letting down any new rain—we finally leave the island, cross over the Stono River on a low, flat bridge, the water we cross edged on both banks by thick marsh gray for the lack of light, the sun's own hand gone, all color washed clean with the coming tide. It's this marsh, the sweetgrass and salt hay and saw grass and pluff mud, all of it, that matters, the way it all seems to converge at water's edge to give the river a kind of soft home, a gentle path toward open sea.

Yet we're still not to Wadmalaw, have only made it to Johns Island, and though there is on this island evidence still of the proud achievements of strip mall manufacturers and mini-mart moguls, there encroaches upon it all the vast feel of the forest, the trees now a looming presence everywhere: live oak, tall pine, sumac with narrow long leaves just turning red for the autumn now upon us. Still the homes and shops retreat, until, in one last gasp, one final threat to all the woods around us, we emerge into a shopping center: a Harris Teeter, a dry cleaner's, a video store, a gas station.

There, on the left across the intersection, this being the last stoplight on Johns—there are none on Wadmalaw, not even in Rockville, the island's only town—is a Circle K. I stop at the light, though there are no cars to be seen, and glance again in the mirror. They're still asleep, Jacob's head leaned to his left, his cheek almost touching his shoulder. Zeb's head is straight back, mouth open wide in a quiet snore.

For a moment I think to wake them, pull into the convenience store, and take orders. But the radio is off, the sky above still that iron gray, and I can see just past the intersection and the Circle K to where there are no more houses, no more minimarts, only a thin two-lane road leading off through live oak to Wadmalaw Island. I see up there, in the darkness of those trees, in the black-green of them, a kind of silence it's hard to find anymore: silence like a treasure, a secret worth the drive out here and whatever wrath my children might wreak upon me once they awaken to no orange soda and M&M's.

The light turns green, and I go, pass the Circle K to my left, head off into the woods.

The bridge over Church Creek is no longer or wider than a good-sized driveway, but once across it we're on Wadmalaw. The water beneath the bridge is flat, a narrow mirror edged in marsh grasses and leading away from either side of the bridge. Then the road leads into those towering live oak, what Zeb called a tree tunnel when he was younger: a heavy canopy of branches thick with Spanish moss; and though it still hasn't rained, huge drops spill from those branches now and again onto the windshield, drops as heavy as mud and as loud, so that I have to put the wipers on Intermittent while beneath them.

Now and again, nestled back inside the woods, sometimes making their way almost to the road, are houses, homes to the workers at the onion and tomato farms out here: haint purple or gray cinder-block or pieced-together clapboard, roofs of rusted tin or green shingles. There are the places of worship, too, for those living here: Mount Zion AME Church and Grace Chapel and New Bethlehem Baptist Church, all of them well-tended and white, carefully cared for, as though the buildings themselves were manifest prayers. Roads, some dirt, some paved, intersect with Maybank, their names secrets themselves, some code to the lives and dreams of those who were born and who have died here: Katy Hill Road, Andros Road, Liberia Road.

I see then up ahead something different about the road, about the shade of gray to the asphalt. It's like there's a silver sheen over the road, shiny and misted as I make my way closer and closer, and too late I realize it's a storm, the rain upon me in only a moment, heavy rain that fills my windshield before I can even slow down, before I can even get the wipers going full blast; and now, too, the silence of the van is shattered by the pounding of the rain, a dark and ominous sound like the drumming of a thousand haints' hands on the roof, and I look in the rearview mirror to see if the noise will awaken the boys, scare them out of sleep.

They don't move, and I see next to me that even the dog has curled up, asleep, on the seat, and now the sound of the rain isn't a noise at all, but a strong and solid reminder of the hand of God, and I wonder, too, how this sound might enter the dreams of my sleeping children, what pictures might play in their heads as a result of the rain on the roof.

The rain stops just as abruptly as it began only moments before, soft wisps of steam rising up off the road before me, and as if in my own dream I see up ahead on the right a widening in the road, beside it a small building worn free of paint, left with only bare boards and old bricks. As I approach I see through the mist an old black man like a specter, red baseball cap on, long-sleeved brown-and-white plaid shirt buttoned to his neck, blue jeans. He's seated on what were the front steps to this building, and only then do I see the old metal sign above the front door, the words almost lost for the rust there: P. M. KING GROCERY, the sign reads, next to the words the Sunbeam Bread logo, and the single word OIL.

Still as though in a dream, the old man raises his hand to me, and I feel my hand rising of its own, see myself wave at this man I do not know, him ready and willing at any moment to wave at a stranger in a gesture I can't help but feel is one of welcome. Then we're gone, the boys and the dog and I, the dream of an old man and an ancient grocery store gone from me, and I'm left with an open road, towering oaks, steam up off the pavement.

As if that ushered me into a different world altogether, the old man an emissary pointing the way to the end of the road and Rockville, the old homes begin appearing. Not shanties but old summer homes of Charleston residents, now inhabited mostly by willing commuters into and out of downtown, the length of the drive more than made up for in the quiet beauty of this place. The homes are white clapboard for the most part, ringed with screened porches and flower gardens, windows framed by black shutters. The oaks are always there, branches always laden with Spanish moss. But rather than showing the intrusive nature of buildings elsewhere on the road here—the strip mall on Johns Island, the drive-thru banks on James—these structures seem easy among the trees, seem almost a part of Wadmalaw Island: Strung between two oaks is a Pawley's Island hammock that seems an invitation to anyone passing by; hung from the branch of a tree at another house is a tire swing. The oaks seem protectors of the houses here, as much like sentinels as the tree tunnel back by Church Creek.

Still more houses appear, each with evidence of its own life: a johnboat lying upside-down in a side yard, its flat bottom and squared-off ends in sharp contrast to the soft jasmine tendrils snaking up a trellis beside the house; a row of crab nets hung from the eaves of a carriagehouse; a tree fort high in the fork of an oak, up the trunk a crooked row of two-by-four pieces nailed by a child's hand.

Finally, like the treasure of silence I've been pursuing, like the culmination of all the secrets this island has shown me, past the red-and-white barrier sign with the words ROAD ENDS in big black letters, lies the marsh, still just as gray as ever this rainy Sunday, beyond it the sound between Wadmalaw and Seabrook Island, that island so close, it seems, I could lean forward and touch it.

I put the van in Park and let the engine idle. There's no preparing for this vista, for the deep breath of air and water and marsh grasses and treeline across the water and low-lying clouds. There is nothing one can do to get ready; all of this is a gift after the long drive out here, though everything I've seen—the water beneath the bridge at Church Creek, the thin mist off wet pavement, even the old man in the baseball cap—has already been gift enough.

I look back to my children, see they are still asleep, Jacob with his head back now, Zeb with his head to one side. I want to wake them. I want them to see this. Yet there is a peace in their sleeping I don't want to interrupt—the chance that they're dreaming of the gift of rain and an afternoon of soccer and M&M's and a black Lab named Willa, nothing I dare to break up.

So instead of waking them I only turn to the water again, the view from Wadmalaw Island, and wait for whatever might happen next. There is nothing, of course. Only the slow twist of marsh grasses in the light wind out there, the lines of the moving tide on the water's surface. Only that.

Then, from high above and behind this all, comes suddenly one last gift: the shift of light down on the world, a tear in the old drab blanket above, a tear that lets down late-afternoon sunlight onto the marsh and sound and island. The marsh is illuminated now, October sunlight spilling down, infusing the once-gray world with wild color, and while I watch, the grasses take on hues and tints of green, a dozen shades of green; and there are browns, too, and bronze and gold and black there in the grass, the island across the silver water lit up as well, the live oaks there an old and heavy and reverent green. And beyond it all, past the island and above the treeline, like a reminder of how short a time these moments of light and beauty last, is a dark granite sky filled with the chance for more rain.

But here, now, beneath this momentary breach in the clouds and in the very fabric of an otherwise lost day, are my children and myself. I cut off the engine then, pop open my door, and climb out, and there comes to me the benevolent surprise of the smell of woods after rain, and the smell, too, of saltwater, and of marsh grass, and of sunlight and gray sky, and yes, even of pluff mud, all of it together a wonderful fragrance in no need of words.

A Sunday, a day of rest, in October on Wadmalaw Island, a day dangerously close to having been lost to television and a rainy sky. Though she does not know it yet, the view from here is the most beautiful gift I can remember Melanie giving me, and already I'm lining up words in my head to give back to her once we drive back home—making certain to stop at the Circle K on Johns Island—words that will amount, I know already, only to a meager translation of all I've seen.

Allegiance

The first time Brad ran away I knew exactly where he was.

I do not know if my parents know this fact even today, as I write this. Such is the depth, I guess, of promises I made to him. "Swear to God," was what he said to me often during our childhood and adolescence. "Swear to God you won't tell Mom," he'd say, then wait for my answer: "I swear." What followed after each promise was a confession designed, I believe, both to impress me and to make me an accessory after—or before—the fact. *Can you believe this is what I'm going to do?* he seemed to be saying, and in the same breath spoke the threat, *Tell, and I'll tell that you knew all along.* Big brothers.

He was at Mark and Marvin Freeman's, two blocks away; they were twin brothers and fellow-freshmen with Brad, and hid him in their garage for a night while my mom and dad stayed up talking to police and calling friends, relatives, anyplace he might show up. After that, once it was too late at night to do anything other than wait for whatever word might come, I watched them split off from each other, my mother going to the window above the kitchen sink, holding herself as she looked out into the black, my father pulling a chair from the dinette set, turning it to the sliding-glass windows onto the rear porch and pool area, their backs to each other. He stared, too, out into the black.

And here I was, possessor of the secret, watching them, dumb with allegiance.

Something happened to Brad when we moved from Buena Park to Phoenix in the middle of his sixth-grade year. Before that he was the big brother everyone knew at Elizabeth Dickerson Elementary. My first days of school each year at Dickerson—I was in the fourth grade when we moved—were ones in which I was identified by nodding teachers as "Brad's brother," followed by the beneficent smile signaling me I'd inherited quite a pleasant legacy, one I never lived up to. Only years later, once I'd finished college and was headed to grad school, did my mom reveal to me her fears for my future back then, fears based on the kinds of grades I used to bring home: She thought I'd wind up bagging groceries at the Bayless, or pumping gas, or end up a middle-aged man washing dishes. Noble endeavors all, just not what a parent wishes on her kids.

But Brad. Brad was a star, a hero: top grades all through elementary, a favorite of everyone. I struggled trying to remember what *indent the beginning of a paragraph* meant—I only know now because a third-grade peer, a Japanese kid whose name I can't recall, explained it to me in terms I could understand: "You start a new part of what you write by going in from the side about as far as the tip of your thumb"—while Brad brought home straight A's.

The day before we moved to Phoenix, Brad's class had a going-away party for him after school, and I remember saying good-bye to my teacher, Miss Craig, a woman whose frosted hair seemed a copper shell atop her head, with nothing more than a "See you later," then going to Brad's classroom, where my mom was waiting for me.

She stood outside the door, and as I came down the covered walkway toward the room, I heard music. Mom opened the door then, and the sound revealed itself: The Monkees, their latest album, one we had at home; the tune "Zilch," though that wasn't a song at all, more a confused swirl of takeoffs on "Revolution No. 9" than anything else. I looked inside.

Here was his entire class, all of them dancing, the desks pushed back to the walls, on one of them the granite gray box of a record player every classroom had. In one corner was a table set up with Dixie cups, beside it a punchbowl filled with what I took to be red Kool-Aid, beside that plates of cookies. Kool-Aid, cookies, kids dancing to the Monkees. They were dancing like what I'd seen on *American Bandstand*, arms all over the place, backs snapping and feet shuffling. They were *dancing* in there.

And there was Brad, leaned back, knees bent, his arms working like slow windmills, him smiling away, dancing.

Then we moved.

Fifteen years later, after a single session in a drug rehab center, Brad would come to our mother's house and inform her everything that had gone wrong with his life was because they'd made him move during the sixth grade. This after an hour with a counselor.

My mother refused this reason. I was there the day after they'd had this talk, and she was still burned up over the blame laid neatly at her and my father's feet. "I told him to look at you!" she shouted at me. "Look at *you*! We moved back to California when you were a junior in high school, I told him, and *you* didn't end up in jail!"

True enough; but now that I've lived here with my own family in one place for the last seven years, and now that Zeb, my older son, is entering fifth grade, believe me when I say we won't be moving anywhere soon.

Because something, in fact, did happen. Though I was in a new school and my life was filled with trying to figure out how to become friends with my classmates, not to mention English and Math and Arizona History and Lore—I was in the fourth grade and still couldn't tell time!—I was aware that something in my brother was breaking down. I cannot pretend to know what happened to him, can only give the litany of events that each seemed crescendo enough, but that would all be eclipsed one way or another somewhere along the line of his life.

It might have started with our next-door neighbor, Lynn, a new kid, just like Brad, who'd moved in a couple of months after we did. Blond-headed, with a motorcycle, a skinny, narrow-chested kid who had a sort of grin that seemed only trouble even to me: his lips never parted, his eyes always halfway closed. He beat me up during a basketball game on our front driveway one afternoon, over an elbow he'd given me to the chest. The only reason I took him on was because Brad was right there, and I thought he'd join me, or pull him away, or stand between us. Something along those lines. But Brad only stood there, my brother, the basketball at his hip, while the kid sat on my arms and punched me in the chest.

The summer after Brad's sixth grade, he and I went out for the swim team at Roadrunner Park, the local community pool and playground. Brad made the team; I was dead last in the one qualifying heat I was in. By the middle of summer Brad had accrued a dozen or so ribbons, most of them blue, in his age class. My mom had them framed, two rows of ribbons hung there on his bedroom wall, proof of his proficiency, that star quality. Practice was at seven o'clock every weekday morning, and Brad rode his bike the mile or so to the park, stayed there until ten, then came home.

But on our way home one morning from the Bayless—the trunk full of groceries, my younger brother, Timmy, and I in the backseat, our baby sister, Leslie, up front with Mom—I felt the car slow down as we drove along 32nd Street, and I saw Mom looking out her window to the desert between the road and Roadrunner Park. I looked out the window, too, saw a few yards off into the scrub and cactus two kids on a motorcycle parallel to us and headed in the same direction we were. Lynn was driving, Brad behind him, his hands to the seat, holding on. They were laughing, passing words back and forth between themselves.

We drove that way, slowly, for a quarter mile or so, my mom all the while glancing from the road to the motorcycle to the road and back, until Lynn peeled the motorcycle off into the brush and away from us. Then she gave it the gas.

Brad came home a little after ten on his bike, his towel

draped over his shoulders, Timmy down the street playing at Cameron's house, Leslie somewhere. I stood in the doorway of my room, listening for what would happen in the kitchen. "How was practice?" Mom said.

"Great," he said. "It was hard." They were silent a few moments, and I heard the refrigerator open up, heard an RC bottle popped open.

Mom said, "We saw you and Lynn riding the motorcycle." Silence again.

Finally Brad said, "That wasn't me. I was in practice."

Though I could see none of this, only heard it from my room, I knew how this scene would play: Brad, once discovered in a lie, never *ever* gave in, as though he actually believed whatever story he could create, actually believed that it was not him we saw twenty yards away, laughing on the back of a motorcycle. I knew, right then, right there, he was looking our mom straight in the eye and telling her it wasn't him.

"I don't think so," Mom said, and I could see her, too, averting her eyes from his, hiding her face as she called him on his lie, as though if she herself were to see his eyes she might actually believe *him*.

"Why don't you believe me, Mom?" he said then, his voice all broken and sorrowful, full of tears. "You never believe me!" He stormed from the kitchen, and I had to duck into my room, not wanting him to know I'd heard it all. His bedroom was across from mine, Timmy and I sharing since we'd moved here. I stood a few feet back inside my room. I heard Brad slam shut his door, waited, waited, then heard him quietly open it.

Here he was, inside our room. He walked right in, his shirt off, wearing cutoffs, the same pair I'd seen him in on the motorcycle. Carefully he closed the door behind him, then turned to me, whispered, "Swear to God you won't tell Mom."

I was quiet no more than a second or two before I nodded, said, "I swear."

"Coach kicked me off the team. He saw me smoking." He looked at me hard, dared me with his eyes not to look away. Of course I did.

Where I'm going with this I do not know, and as I type this on the computer, my younger son, Jacob, stands beside me at my old manual typewriter, set up on the desktop, the typewriter I wrote my first three books on, a beat-up Brother portable I got for high school graduation. He'd not seen it before this afternoon. We're headed to Vermont for the summer, and since I can't fit my computer into the van, it's my plan to bring the manual, hope for the best.

"Maaaan!" he said when he saw it on my desk, as though it were the latest in computer hardware, this thing you have to slam at to get the keys to print, an arm out to the side you have to pull on quick and hard to get the carriage back into place. Pure technology, he thinks. Now I want to show him how it works, and so I type out:

Jacob Daynes Lott was born on December 10, 1985, just
15 days before Christmas, making him the best Christmas
present I ever got.

He smiles when he sees it, then reads it out loud to me. I pull the carriage return a couple of times, look at him, and say, "There. You can type whatever you want."

He looks at it, bites on his lower lip, grins. He points his index finger, searches out the keys. "Press hard," I say, "or it won't print dark enough." He finds the key he wants, then puts his finger to it, taps hard. The letter *Z* appears, a little light, but there.

Z for Zeb, I know. His older brother. He types, me pressing the shift key when needed, and I watch as he spells out the words, "Zeb Lott was born on May 12, 1983." The print is still a little light, almost empty in places. But it is a sentence, readable. I turn back to my work, let him type beside me while I keep going.

Still, vestiges of Brad's waning glory surfaced now and again, as when, in the spring of the seventh grade, he was cast by Mrs. Gentry, our music teacher—our school ran from kindergarten to eighth grade—in the role of Pigpen for the school's production of *You're a Good Man, Charlie Brown*. He was a good singer, he could act. I'd seen him in rehearsals, little more than people standing around in the music room, what made it the music room the presence of a piano in one corner. But he was good.

A week before the play was to open over at the high school, Brad was kicked off the cast. He'd decided one day to go out in the desert with Lynn and a couple other guys to hunt ground squirrels instead. I watched him from the kitchen window walking off down the driveway with two chlorine bottles filled with water for the hunt: You followed a squirrel toward its hole, and when it disappeared inside, you poured a gallon of water down in there, waited for the thing to float up. Sometimes it escaped out another entry; sometimes, there it was.

But before he left with the bottles in tow, he said to me, "Swear to God you won't tell Mom what we're doing." I swore.

The afternoon my mom got the call from Mrs. Gentry, Brad cried to her, "She hates me, she hates me! That's why she kicked me out!" then stormed to his room, slammed shut that door yet again.

I turn to Jacob to see what it is he's been typing the last ten minutes or so. I look over his shoulder, ready to smile at my second son's writing, be it story or gibberish, whatever it is.

After the news of his big brother's birthday is the unfinished sentence, "Though in these days I don,t like him very much but I still"

"What are you typing that for?" I say, too loud, already angry at him. Here he is at a typewriter for the first time, banging out a message about how much he doesn't like his big brother in these days.

"I was just—," he starts, but I cut him off, say, "You love your brother. You love him. You don't stand here and type about how you don't like him."

The irony of the entire scene is lost on me for a few minutes: The huge and ugly line drawn between what I have at that moment been writing about my older brother and what my son has been writing about *his* older brother is too big, a plank in my eye while I holler on about the speck in my son's.

Jacob walks in his sleep nearly every night. One night last week we found him walking down the hallway toward his brother's room, the top sheet from his bed trailing behind him, a corner of it held tight in a fist. "Zeb," he was saying, his eyes half opened and glazed with sleep. "I have to tell Zeb," he said again, his mind always so deeply set on his brother and what he is doing at any given moment that, even in sleep, he's preoccupied with him.

Yesterday morning Zeb came downstairs for breakfast and stretched, yawned as he sat at the table. "I slept really good last night," Zeb said.

Jacob, already at the table, a spoonful of Froot Loops up and headed for his mouth, stopped, looked first to Zeb, then to his mom. "I slept better," he said.

I realize now, with Jacob's sleepwalking to his brother's room, with that small sentence banged into a manual typewriter, with his measuring his entire world against only his brother, Jacob is me, just trying to make my way in the wake, for better or worse, of big brother Brad.

Where to from here with this tale of my older brother's fall from grace? His running away that first time might seem the next logical step, though there are any number of incidents I could talk about: the two times he was arrested for possession of marijuana; the two cars he totaled, one while our parents were away in Las Vegas, Mom's last words as she followed Dad out the door: "Brad, don't drive the car"; the second time he ran away, this time by flying to San Diego with Bruce Homer, the two of them sophomores, where they would spend what little money they had quickly, end up sleeping on the beach before Bruce would wise up, call home, get money wired for bus fare back, while Brad, invincible in his resolve, would not give in, only hitch his way up the coast to my grandparents in the San Fernando Valley, where he would spend the summer working as a janitor alongside my grandpa at Consolidated Film Industries; the telegram from Brad's commander on the *U.S.S. Tolovana* when Brad was arrested in Yokohama for bringing marijuana on board, the stash hidden inside his scuba tanks, the telegram simply stating he was confined to the ship for the duration of the cruise; the annulment of his first marriage; the addiction.

And of my ascendence, my rise in the face of his fall? For me there was marching band, church membership, jobs at Taco Bell and Smith's Food King and Knott's Berry Farm and RC Cola, the senior prom, the president's list for a 4.0 GPA in college, a marriage still intact, graduate school, a professorship, and publications.

Where to, except to ask why this difference between brothers exists, brothers raised in the same household, by the same parents?

Of course there is no answer. Only that we are different people. It would be pleasant, comforting—perhaps that drug rehab counselor's only aim, really, was to comfort Brad with a place to lay blame—to believe it boiled down to a move in the sixth grade; but the truth stares at me so evident, so plain it might as well be a plank in my eye: We are two people.

What I know now, though, is the true nature of my question, and why I ask it: I am a father, afraid for my children and the lives out there gearing up to swallow them whole. I want to find how the lives of my children can take their turns away from me, just as Brad's took its turn from my parents, so I might stay this from happening in my own sons' lives.

Here are my parents, staring out windows, their backs to each other, wondering where their firstborn has gone, and why.

Brad turned up at school the next day, simply rode the bus in with the Freeman boys. My mother was called—Dad was, by no choice other than to make a living, at work—and she drove to school, where Brad was in the principal's office.

When she asked why he'd done it, he shrugged, said, "I don't know." He was smiling, my mother told me this afternoon when I called her for just this, to find out what it was like as a parent to discover your runaway son has returned. Brad was smiling in the principal's office, pleased with himself for what power he'd exerted in all this.

This was my mother's assessment of the situation. And I remember seeing Brad come home that afternoon from school —I was still at Greenway Junior High then, and got home before he did—I remember him coming into the house, the bus that'd dropped him off at the corner long gone, my mother silent as he entered, pulling from the refrigerator a bottle of RC, then adjourned himself to his room, gently closing that door.

But not before looking at me leaning out of my own doorway, his eyes speaking the same old threat: *Tell, and I'll tell that you knew all along.* I did not tell, not even this afternoon, instead asked my mother about what it was like to have a son run away, me still dumb with allegiance. Such is the power of a big brother.

"Don't tell Dad," I heard Zeb whisper to Jake from the playroom one afternoon not long ago. I was here, in my office, working away at a short story: my sales pitch, a son after his father's heart, in my own way.

"Jake, don't tell Dad," Zeb whispered, and it seemed *Swear to God you won't tell* ought to be the next words I would hear.

Is it any wonder, then, that I left my desk and headed for the playroom, bent on finding out what matters of secrecy had been placed in motion, bent on the sad hope, for better or worse, of breaking the allegiance between brothers?

It was only a matter, finally, of the soccer ball being bounced against the playroom wall. And it was Zeb to confess, Jacob, his little brother, already dumb with allegiance. But what else could I have done?

Royal Crown 2

I bought my first car from, of course, one of the men at RC, a sales supervisor by the name of Roger Pedley, a man from Minnesota who wore his hair in a huge pompadour perched atop his forehead and who spoke so tight-lipped it seemed he never opened his mouth. By the end of that summer I had enough saved to buy the car, a '49 Chevrolet four-door with, believe it or not, only twenty-two thousand miles on it. The car had belonged to his mother back in Minnesota, and she only drove it to get groceries and to go to church on Sundays. Really.

So even my primary teenage rite of passage—ownership of a car—was indelibly stamped with an association to RC Cola; and it was in that car that Brad, who was home on leave, back from the first of his three SEAPAC cruises, Tim, and I drove back to California in February 1975. Our father, transferred back to the land of flowing soda in gutters, drove the brown Ford LTD in front of us for five hundred miles, with my mother and baby sister, Leslie, the driver, our dad, promoted to vice president of the Los Angeles franchise of RC Cola.

Gone, of course, were the boys' jobs at RC, the Phoenix franchise a podunk operation in comparison, my dad able easily to pass us off on the payroll back there. The Los Angeles franchise was the big time, tied into national headquarters in Chicago. I'd gotten a taste for work in all those summers, and a taste for the accompanying money, so the summer after my junior year I found a job at Knott's Berry Farm, where I made candy apples in Food Services, got up at five-fifteen five days a week, weekends among them, then drove up Beach Boulevard from Huntington Beach all the way to Buena Park in the dark. There I skewered a couple hundred apples each day, dipped them two at a time into a large vat of red syrup I'd cooked up, then set them out to cool.

My friends—the small cadre I'd accrued in the few months we'd lived there—thought I was nuts getting up that early, especially during summer vacation. What they didn't know, of course, was my history, the way my dad had called my name out at this exact time every summer morning for the last three years, the way it'd been ingrained in me, this notion of work, this getting up early to go and make your way in this world. And besides, I was off work by one-thirty each day, still had plenty of time to head to the beach.

And strangely, too, I looked forward to getting up, to doing this job, because my father hadn't arranged any of it, hadn't fixed things for me, and wasn't there, a looming presence, in all I did. I wasn't the boss's son, wasn't handed the job, wasn't driven there by my dad. I still stopped on occasion at the Winchell's donut shop on Beach on my way in, had a donut or two—they didn't have bear claws—and a milk, as though that ritual itself were a part of waking up, gearing up for the day ahead: all those apples, all those skewers, that vat of bubbling candy.

I ended up working there through that summer and into the fall, going part-time Saturdays and Sundays once school started; I kept on, too, through Christmas and into the spring of my senior year, so that every Saturday and Sunday I was out of the house by five-thirty, every week bringing home a paycheck, every Friday night spending all of it on my girlfriend and movies and dinner and whatever else it is you waste money on your senior year of high school, so that when I got accepted into the forestry program at Northern Arizona University and there lay before me only twelve weeks to make enough money to last me a whole year—me with all my money spent and a job skewering apples at $3.10 an hour—I had no choice but to accept my dad's offer of summer employment at good old RC Cola. There I would make $5 an hour, have weekends off, could drive in with him so I wouldn't have to put miles on my car or pay any gas. Attractive, to say the least.

At five-fifteen the morning after I graduated high school, me up until three the night before, my dad leaned into my room, called my name, said, "Time to get up."

On Beach Boulevard, headed for the 405, then the Harbor Freeway and the ride into Watts, where the RC plant was, my dad slowed down, put on his right blinker, eased the car into a parking lot.

Before us stood a donut shop—an independent, not a part of a chain like Winchell's—a donut shop I hadn't seen those mornings driving in to Knott's. Dad climbed out, and I followed him to the window; there was no waiting room here, no inside place from which to order. You only stood at the window, ordered, paid.

They had bear claws.

I spent the summer building racks, those huge wooden structures you see on the ends of aisles in grocery stores, under the direction of one Jimmy Galintino, a short, gray-haired man who'd been with the company for thirty years and whose ears stuck out from his head like the handles on a trophy. I was in the middle of Watts in a sprawling factory, hundreds of people at work in all the adjacent buildings, the bottling line running twenty-four hours a day nonstop. Mr. Galintino spent his days in the air-conditioned comfort of his office: yet another shack, this one set up inside the warehouse, a room within a room, where he filled out rack orders, called stores and arranged times for new racks to be delivered, old ones to be picked up, while I sat outside, the pieces of these things spread out around me like the bones of a big dead animal waiting for me to reassemble them.

Once enough of them were built, we loaded them onto the back of a flatbed truck and drove away, headed all over Southern California, from San Clemente to Ventura, Pasadena to San Pedro, Simi Valley to San Bernardino. We spent a lot of time together, just driving on freeways, me riding shotgun while Mr. Galintino drove, behind us the racks I'd put together, lashed down tight.

He talked, his words quick and loud, his hands working all the while, me afraid we were going to rear-end somebody at any minute. He was barely able to see over the steering wheel, and spent his drive time imparting the history of Royal Crown Cola to me as though he were some sort of oracle, me his amanuensis, though all I ever did was nod, look out my window, wonder which Vons we were headed for, where we might get lunch.

He told me of how he'd been the one to invent the display tray, the fold-up and precut sheet of cardboard in which product was placed, to build displays of RC or Diet Rite or anything else; he told me of when Nehi was king and you couldn't give away RC; he told me of the first summer they sold a million cases out of the Los Angeles franchise, and of when he was a driver and it was so hot one day that bottles were exploding in the bays.

He told me, too, of the Watts riots, and how he and a couple other men had had to sit up on the roof with guns in order to keep people from looting the factory, told me of an RC truck burned to the ground for no good reason other than that the truck had been there, an easy target. He told me of snipers on the roofs of other buildings taking potshots at trucks as they pulled in that first late afternoon that all the trouble started, and told me of how he, of course, hadn't fired his gun, only made his presence known with a few of the other fellows, there on the roof of the bottling line.

He'd known my dad for years, he said, knew him back when he was doing driver-truck sales for the company, then when Dad had become the first pre-salesman. Back in the fifties the notion of sending someone in to take an order and having it delivered off the truck by somebody else the next day was as radical as you could get, Mr. Galintino let me know. My dad was something of a mover, he let me know, a man who could sell ice to

Eskimos, brimstone to the devil, kosher beef to Arabs; and he let me know, too, how proud I ought to be of Dad, how great a man he was.

And he told me of how my father, the story legendary in the annals of Royal Crown, had gotten into a fistfight with a Coke salesman once, a fight right there in the soda-pop aisle of a Safeway in Long Beach, a fight over who had the right to which facings on the shelf.

"Who won?" I asked when he was through with the story.

He looked at me, his hands finally still and in place on the steering wheel. It was a look that seemed to size me up, and seemed to find me wanting. He smiled, shrugged. "Doesn't matter, does it?" he said.

I took all these stories as being an old man's attempts at brownnosing the boss's son, though I never let on I felt this way. I only worked alone building racks in a warehouse not much different from those at the plant in Phoenix. All this history, handed to me, a willing but unwilling compatriot. I bore him no ill will, except when he came out of his office and told me to hurry it up with the racks, that I wasn't moving fast enough. But I liked him, liked him for how loud he was, for how he slapped salesmen on the back when we ran into them out on calls; liked him even for the way he moved his hands when he drove, as though in these moves I was brought closer to the story, saw him punch the bastard who stole his first few trays and made a fortune out of the idea, saw the rifle in his hands as he sighted down Slauson Avenue.

So much history, but all of it, I thought, wasted on me. I

was only marking time, getting my paycheck and drinking my RC while waiting for the day I'd drive off for Flagstaff, Arizona, and the real life that lay before me. I was going to be a forest ranger, had planned since my first days in Boy Scouts and camping on the Mogollin Rim to spend my life riding a horse, helping people make certain their campfires were out, this sort of thing. RC, of course, was my father's life, the way he'd made his way in this world. Not me; so when on a late August morning in 1976 I got into my car, a yellow Ford LTD, an ex-company car my dad had sold me, me convinced by Dad that the old Chevy wouldn't make it across the desert and back again, I knew RC and all the hours I'd ever worked there were long behind me, in my pocket a cashier's check, that pot of cash I'd saved all summer long the only proof of my association with the place.

Along with the two RC towels I had, those big beach towels I wanted to use for after showers. And there was the car, too. And the RC duffel bag. But past that, RC was gone.

Until I moved back at the end of fall semester.

Forestry, it turned out, was product yields, computer models, soil tests. Everything but riding a horse. And my girlfriend was back home, too.

The day after Christmas, at six A.M. sharp, I pulled up to the branch sales office in Lynwood, a low building with a small parking lot out front, the lot crammed with cars. I had on my RC company shirt, light blue with the logo stitched above the left breast pocket; had on the wide blue RC tie I'd borrowed from my dad, the one with the tiny logo centered on the bottom tip. I had on my navy blue polyester company pants. I had on my RC Eisenhower jacket, the logo stitched on its left breast, too, and had on my black steel-toed shoes, my navy socks. My dad'd brought the clothes home for me even before I got back from Flagstaff.

I had to park ten or twelve cars down from the front door of the place, and sat there with the headlights on, trying to figure out what was going to happen. I hadn't done this before, hadn't been simply sent alone to an RC outpost. Eighteen years old, I wanted my dad there with me.

I cut the lights, opened the door, and climbed out. There were still stars out, I remember, as I moved for the door, scared to death of what might happen once I entered: People would look at me, wonder who I was, why I was here. *The boss's son,* they would think, *some wuss forced on us by the big man downtown.*

I put my hand to the knob, pushed open the door. Light from inside fell out onto the ground before me, and I looked up, saw precisely what I'd feared I'd find: thirty or forty men, all dressed as I was, seated at tables, all of them looking straight at me. At the far end of the room stood a small, thick man in a white dress shirt, his tie not a company tie but wild swirls of color. His hair was slicked back on his head, his ears from the same mold as Mr. Galintino's. He held a cigarette in one hand, took a drag. Con Andros, branch manager. The man who'd hired me in an all-but-pro-forma interview last week. A man of goodwill, I believed. A nice man. A good man.

In the silence of all these men watching me, he said, "Mr. Lott, good afternoon. Glad you could make it."

The branch was in a meeting, and I eased myself in the door, moved along the wall to my left, and leaned against it,

tried not to be seen, even with these men looking at me. I nodded, tried to smile, crossed my arms.

"Mr. Lott," he went on, smiling as he spoke, "when we say
be here at six o'clock, it means that's when the festivities begin.
Be here by six o'clock, means, in all actuality, *be here by five-forty-
five.* Am I understood?" He took another drag off the cigarette,
held in the smoke, smiled at me.

I could see the other men smiling, too. "Yes, sir," I said.

"Fine," he said. "Wonderful." He breathed out the smoke,
said, "And welcome to our humble shop."

At the meeting I was introduced to "fact sheets," flyers of a sort,
advertising upcoming sale prices on product; salesmen give
these out to grocery store managers in order to get them to buy
displays. And I was introduced to the sales board, one whole
wall of the room, a huge grid displaying numbers and names of
all the products sold: RC, Diet Rite, Schweppes, Nehi, RC100,
Mug Root Beer. Each day the salesmen posted their sales, wrote
the numbers in green if they were above projection, in red if
they were below, so that everyone in the branch knew who was
selling what, and knew, too, whose job was secure, whose wasn't.

After the meeting I was ushered by one of the salesmen out
into the warehouse behind the sales meeting room, and to the
P.O.P. room. There I was issued a cardboard case, given a few
rolls of Day-Glo stickers advertising prices on RC and Diet Rite
and Schweppes; there I was given stacks of carton stuffers and
bottle hangers, all Day-Glo. There I was issued a price gun, a
plastic thing that looked a little like some hand-held weapon

from *Star Wars* but that only fed out paper price labels when you pulled the trigger. Garveys were ancient history.

And there I was issued a feather duster.

I spent the duration of the Christmas break, through to the end of January, driving around in my car to grocery stores all over Orange County and the South Bay, where I merchandised the shelves, writing on the backs of carton stuffers the number of cases I would need of what in order to fill the shelves, then heading to the back rooms, those dark caverns, and wheeling out product, filling the shelves, putting up P.O.P. On occasion I stopped, talked to stock clerks about those Lakers, the prospects for the Dodgers, how the Rams had blown it in the playoffs.

What more can be said about the role of Royal Crown in my life, except that it became evident on that morning that somehow I would end up in this life, though I kept making forays into other worlds of work? I enrolled at Cal State Long Beach for the spring semester as a marine biology major for no good reason I can recall other than that I liked the ocean; that semester I got a job working as a fry cook at a CoCo's in Newport Beach, given the job because of my veteran experience with Food Services at Knott's Berry Farm. I never told them that that experience amounted only to the dipping of apples into hot candy. That semester I flunked Ocean Fishing, a PE course I got tired of and simply quit going to; that semester I got engaged to my girlfriend, then broke up with her.

And that summer I went right back to RC for more merchandising work and, toward the end of the summer, vacation-relief sales, yet another rung or so up the corporate ladder. Here I was given the route sales book of one of the men, then followed his route, called on managers with my fact sheets, and tried to sell to them. I was a tentative salesman, willing only to hand a manager a sheet, say a few words about a possible endcap I'd spotted down there, off the bread aisle, or here, up front, next to the produce area. Then I'd disappear into the back room, take inventory, pencil out an order sheet that would bring in just enough cases to fill the rows, just enough to cover what I'd put up on the shelf.

In the fall, still a marine biology major, I worked at a restaurant called the Big Yellow House in Costa Mesa, given the job based on my veteran experience with CoCo's. I never told them my expertise amounted to frying up onion rings and french fries; never told them, either, of the fire I'd started in the cook station after I left a pile of wicker baskets, the ones they serve onion rings in, on top of the deep-fryer exhaust pipe, never told them about the manager spraying down the fryer with a fire extinguisher, then turning to me, his face dusted with the white powder. I only shrugged.

The Big Yellow House was a restaurant that featured American food: pot roast and fried chicken and barbecued ribs, mashed potatoes and creamed corn and green beans, all of it served up family style. That is, waitresses in granny dresses brought out big plates heaped with food and set them on the table; you were left to serve yourself. There was a feature to the restaurant, too, that seemed pretty clever at the time but now only seems the gimmick it was: Kids ate based on what they weighed; in the front room of the place children had to step up on an old-fashioned scale, watch the needle spin around until it landed on a certain price.

I ended up working there through Christmas break, ended up, too, being promoted to the opening crew of the chain itself, and spent the next spring training cooks to cook for the company at a new restaurant opening up in Brea, a good forty minutes inland from Huntington Beach. There I preached the subtleties of cayenne pepper in the creamed corn, the art of pot roast cooked in coffee, the beatific ramifications of ribs cooked until the meat just fell from the bone.

This was when, too, I moved out, left the confines of my parents' house for the grown-up world of a rental home shared with three other guys, friends I'd met at church: two surfers, one seminary student. I worked late at the restaurant, often didn't make it home until two-thirty or three o'clock, then got up and went to classes at Cal State the next morning. Though my grades stayed up, for the most part, there entered my life a course called Elementary Physics, a required course for all marine biology majors, a course in which you had to receive a *C* or better in order to remain a marine biology major.

I did not pass.

But this fact did not seem to muddy up my life, not in the least: I was working on the opening crew for a chain of restaurants the success of which was assured; four new stores were opening up, one in Anaheim, one in Carson, one in Bakersfield, another in Cedar Rapids; I was living in a house I helped pay for; I was keeping my own hours, responsible for myself and my way in this world. Convinced, certainly, that this restaurant business was my future. *Who I was.*

Which is why I told the vice-president of the Big Yellow House, Inc., that I was the one who ought to be made assistant manager of the store in Brea. They'd just fired the assistant for stealing meat out of the reefer, and as I surveyed my life, saw all I had going for me, saw the way even this failing of a physics course had serendipitously landed me out of school and in the corporate good hands of the restaurant chain, I came to see this, in fact, was my destiny: me, a restaurateur.

No, the VP said. I was only nineteen, and had to be twenty-one for reasons involving the lounge, where drinks were served while you waited for a table.

I'll quit if you don't let me be assistant manager, I told him, me there in a cook's smock and apron, the two of us standing in the cook station while my trainees served up perfectly rendered versions of corporate recipes: salisbury steak, mashed potatoes and gravy, those ribs.

Then quit, he said.

That weekend, astounded by the company's lack of vision, which was coupled, of course, with the ugly irony of the fact I'd dropped out of school, certain of the company's visionary capacity—*of* course *they would hire me as assistant manager!*—I went over to Mom and Dad's for dinner, a weekly routine that involved me cooking up steaks out on the patio for the entire family, since I was the one who knew so much about cooking. Each Sunday my dad made it a point to holler to me from inside, "Don't burn the steaks!" Each Sunday I stood with my head tilted to one side and breathed out a sigh such as only a nineteen-year-old shown the obvious by his all-knowing father can sigh.

But this Sunday he came out and watched me cook up the

steaks while I told him of what had happened, about the idiocy of the company. I was a good worker, I told him, showed up on time, did what was asked, knew how to get things done.

"Work for RC," he said. "Weekends free. No nights. Base salary and commission. Nickel a case." He paused, said, "Brad's on the table-set crew. Timmy's building racks for Galintino." He paused again. "Weekends free," he said. "Nickel a case." I remember taking in a breath then, looking over at him. He only watched the steaks, his hands on his hips, waiting.

I sat down on the porch swing, tongs in hand. Above me was the latticework of the patio roof, the afternoon light broken into long lines and shadows that lay across my legs like something trying to cut me in pieces, or something trying to mend me. I heard the steaks cooking along with no help from me, just sizzling there on the grill. I smelled the smoke.

My dad, my towering father who, in fact, was three inches shorter than me by then, stood looking at the steaks, his eyes creased closed for the smoke.

Here was RC.

Here was my life.

No surprise.

He said, "You're not going to let these burn, are you?" and looked at me, smiled.

I was a salesman, full-blown. Five company-issue shirts, five pairs of pants. A tie, a car allowance, a trunk full of P.O.P. and cardboard trays. A permanent nametag, BRET LOTT etched in plastic, white letters on a blue background, above the name the RC logo. A route sales book, a route.

I told all my friends it was a good decision, told them I could see myself doing this for the rest of my life. I told this to my parents, told this to my housemates. I told this to myself, too, whenever I pulled up at a Vons or Ralphs or Stater Brothers: *This is a good decision, I can see myself doing this for the rest of my life.*

My route was made up of beach communities: Newport Beach, Corona del Mar, Balboa Island; Costa Mesa was in there, too, and parts of Santa Ana and Fountain Valley, all of it in Orange County. Out of the house before daylight, pulling up the driveway past dark most nights.

The afternoon of my fourth day, a Thursday, I pulled into a Vons on Harbor Boulevard in Costa Mesa, parked the car, went around to the trunk. I popped it open, loaded what I needed from the trunk into the cardboard case I carried with me into each store: all that P.O.P., my price gun, a few cardboard trays to fill out a display. I pulled out my duster, poked the handle into my back pocket. I walked in, went to the shelf, wrote down on the back of a carton stuffer what I needed to fill. I went into the back room, rounded up a hand truck, made my way past pallets stacked with sacks of dog food and boxes of bleach to the soda-pop area, then loaded up what I needed.

After I'd filled the shelf, I put up the P.O.P.—"You want to roll out the proverbial red carpet!" Con Andros had exhorted me at a meeting last Friday afternoon, before I went on route by myself—a bottle hanger on every other bottle; a carton stuffer in every six-pack, there in the slot for the center bottle.

When I was done I made my way up to the courtesy booth at the front of the store. I had my route sales book open, saw at the top of the sales card for the store the manager's name, Allen

Shenck, and started rehearsing my introduction: *Hi! I'm Bret Lott, your new RC salesman, and I just wanted to give you this fact sheet on RC two-liters . . .*

I passed between two empty check stands, made it to the wood and smoked glass of the courtesy booth. An older man in a shirt and tie and red Vons vest, his white hair perfectly coiffed and lacquered into place, stood inside on the raised floor of the booth. He was looking down at me, his head leaned to one side, arms crossed, ready, I could see, for whatever pitch he knew was coming.

"Is Mr. Schenk here?" I said, smiling.

"You're looking at him," he said. He leaned his head the other way.

"Hi!" I said, and felt myself blush a moment. I put out my hand to him. He reached over the glass partition between us and down to my hand, took it, gave it one quick shake. He crossed his arms again, all without taking his eyes off me.

I said, "I'm Bret Lott, your new RC salesman, and I just wanted—"

"What's your name?" he cut in, and I saw him glance at my nametag. He uncrossed his arms, put his hands up to the glass, hooked his fingers over the top edge, holding it.

"Bret Lott," I said. "I just wanted—"

"You're not related to that other Lott down there—Bill— are you?" Still he held on to the glass. He was looking at me.

"Yes," I said, and tried to smile, not sure where this was going. "He's my dad," I said.

This Mr. Schenk's mouth dropped open a moment, then snapped shut. He blinked once, twice. "Good God," he said, his voice too loud, and I wondered what the stock clerks within earshot would think, the new kid in the store already raising the ire of their manager.

"Good God," he said again, then slowly shook his head. "Bill used to be my salesman," he said, and looked down, hands still on the glass, head still shaking.

I know I shocked him, this second-generation salesman from RC showing up to peddle still more soda pop to him, Allen Schenk, still a manager after all these years. But I think the shock to me was just as great as it was to him. Here I was: the RC man.

I believe I smiled, then nodded, said, "Pleased to meet you."

I lasted a year on the route before what I had told myself and told others was simply something I could no longer believe: *This is a good decision, I can see myself doing this for the rest of my life.* I was a good salesman, sold displays, filled shelves, beat my projection for the entire year, more green numbers than red on the sales board. Every Sunday afternoon at my parents' house my dad talked to us boys of Royal Crown, my father holding court, making the rounds of topics: first me and the Schweppes promotion coming up at Christmas; next Brad, and how the table set at the Gelson's up in Newport Hills had gone, whether we'd been buried in facings by Coke or not; finally, little brother Timmy, a swamper for RC now, riding shotgun on trucks out of the Lynwood office, Dad's questions to him more about how the trucks were performing and if the dispatcher, Ted Blankenship, was doing his best at routing out the stops.

But inside that year there came to me the belief in something else for me, something that involved going back to school, finishing a degree, whatever it was in, because I'd come, slowly and fully, to hate what I was doing. Every day you had to walk into a store and talk a manager, a man who thought very little of you in the first place, thought of you as more of a pest than anything else, thought of you as a *salesman*, into buying something people really didn't need in the first place.

But even that reason, I see only now as I write this down, is a ploy, a way to hide behind the real truth of why I didn't want to stay a salesman. No, I see now, it wasn't the nature of the product that made me decide to abandon this life I'd seen for myself, this good decision. It was simply the fact of placing who I was on the line every minute I was inside the store. You became someone new, someone else, when you walked in, whether it was before dawn at your first stop, a huge Albertson's, the store not yet open, the intercom blasting Aerosmith throughout the store, stock clerks dressed in ragged shirts and beat-up jeans throwing product onto the shelves, hauling ass to get the aisles cleared before the first customers showed up at seven-thirty; or whether it was the last stop on Tuesday, mom-and-pops day, this last store a Korean dairy in Garden Grove, a mom-and-pop if ever there was one, complete with a kimchee burial plot out back, seven children huddled around a milk crate turned over and being used as a dinner table, Pop nodding at you, smiling, inviting you to partake of his meal, on your mind only the ten-case stack you wanted to sell him in the hopes of meeting your projection that day.

You were someone else.

I was someone else.

True stories, all of this.

I could do this no longer, could not give up my self upon entry into the marketplace. Not because there was anything wrong with it, or because there was any deceit inside it. I simply did not like it. Plain and simple.

So I enrolled that spring in a night class at Golden West Community College, just took a class, any class I could find, in order to prepare myself for getting back in the saddle that fall: I'd already re-enrolled at Cal State. I took a course that sounded interesting, sounded fun. Creative writing was the name of the thing, and I had no idea what to expect.

Things fall apart, and find their own ends, finally, in ways we cannot imagine, ways that defy precisely what we imagined in the first place.

I have no doubt my father imagined, on those mornings when he held out to his three sons soda pop with the caps already off—have no doubt he saw in the way we ran across the asphalt driveway and across his freshly mowed lawn and to the curb, saw in the way three boys knelt to the concrete gutter, smiling, laughing, careful with each bottle, that he was bestowing something good on them, something to save, something with which to build their lives, though perhaps he did not think of it in this way, thought perhaps he was only letting them have some of the fun involved in the job: fizzy colors and two-cent redemptions.

And I have no doubt he imagined for us, later in our lives, careers with the company. It was the safest—and only—life he had known, a company man since 1953, when he was hired on at age eighteen to drive truck for Nehi, a life safe enough for his children, secure enough for our own lives.

But what I know he could not imagine was the way in which these lives played themselves out, the way in which events out of our hands became events looming in our lives, events bearing down hard on us, forcing turns we had no idea we might ever make:

He was fired from RC in 1980, twenty-seven years after he'd started with the company; fired because when a new president was named and moved down from Chicago to take over the branch, this man found inside the hearts of the men who worked both for and with my father a sort of allegiance that he knew he could not inherit: Bill, my dad, vice president, knew the buyers at all the corporate headquarters, had known them for decades; had known them all since he was that salesman, themselves those stock clerks winking at us those Saturday afternoons we followed our towering father into the stores, feather dusters in our back pockets; Bill, my dad, knew the inside of his own company, too, knew everyone from the branch managers right on down to the swampers.

They all knew him, and knew him to be the RC man, the one they could count on, that same man who'd made himself legendary for punching it out with a Coke salesman in a Safeway in Long Beach over who would get how many facings, that same man who'd been the first pre-salesman in soda pop history, the same man who'd singlehandedly turned the Phoenix franchise into a moneymaker.

The same man who'd wanted for me this life, the life of becoming someone new upon entering a store.

He was fired, given no notice, only told to leave, here is your severance pay, thank you very much. Within the week he was hired on by Dr. Pepper in the same capacity, his value duly noted by the competition all these years.

And the sales force started leaving, salesman after salesman after salesman giving notice at RC, hiring on at Dr. Pepper, until this movement, this immigration, became so apparent to the new president that he informed my father at a dinner given by one of the store chains that he would fire me, Bill's son the salesman—the salesman with his eye on the door already, already enrolled at Cal State—if Dad kept hiring men away from RC.

"Go ahead, fire him," my dad told him, and I can see the smile on his face, the dare there, but the faith, too, I hope, that his son could fend for himself. Or start up with DP. "He's a big boy," my dad told the president.

And I was fired.

The next week I got a job as a reporter for the *Daily Commercial News*, a shipping newspaper based in Lynwood. I made fifty dollars more a week, worked from eight-thirty to five o'clock. And worked with words, wrote and wrote and wrote. I'm glad for my father's dare.

Brad split, headed to Colorado once his first marriage had been annulled on the grounds of fraud. There he lived in Aspen and worked as a bar boy in one of the glamor pads up there, making no money but living in Colorado. A few months later he split yet again, this time for the Gulf of Mexico, where he put his machinist's mate's expertise to good use on an oil rig out past the horizon.

Then he came home, back to California, where he worked as a photographer's assistant, managing even to put together a few catalogs on his own, industrial work but work all the same. He is a good photographer. Several of his prints hang in my home, now, here.

Now, too, he is a Sheetrock man, married with two daughters and working in Sequim, Washington, where he and his family live in a trailer set up on a parcel of land they bought; he has plans to build a house himself, stick by board, and I have no doubt he will do this. Hard work.

Timmy hung in the longest, stayed first with Dr. Pepper, working as a merchandiser hired by my father. Then, when he'd worked his way up to a salesman himself, his route Santa Ana and Irvine, Mission Viejo and El Toro, Dr. Pepper was bought out by Coke, and he was then a Coke salesman, working for the same company my father'd brawled with all those years ago in a Safeway.

He stayed a salesman for nine years, until one morning a year or so ago a supervisor in a sales meeting told the men to leave their integrity in the car. "I don't care who you are," this supervisor said. "You want the sale, you get it whatever way you can. Leave your integrity in the car."

My brother called me that evening, told me of these words, and told me of how suddenly he looked around him, at the other men all dressed as he himself was dressed, and resolved in that moment to quit, to quit as soon as he could.

"But I haven't told Dad," he told me, too. "I don't know what he'd do."

"Why don't you tell him?" I said, as though I didn't already know the answer.

He was quiet awhile, the line between us, from his coast to

mine, as quiet and crisp as a morning before daylight, stars above you as you head in to work.

"Because," he finally started. "Because all my life," he said, "I've done what he wanted me to. All my life I've wanted to make him happy."

I said nothing, and knew what he meant.

He quit anyway, finally given the nerve, I believe, simply by the conviction in his heart of his own integrity. He, too, found a job he enjoys, now designs and sells playground equipment from Orange County all the way to Las Vegas. Hard work.

When Coke took over Dr. Pepper, my dad lost his job again, squeezed out once more. After that he started working for a food brokerage firm, a company that sells product from the manufacturer to the chains. He sells anything and everything—sacks of dog food, boxes of bleach, pallets of toilet paper—and has called me on more than a few occasions to inform me of a particularly large sale: "Sold four freight cars of detergent," he once told me over the phone.

Not what he had imagined on a Saturday morning in Buena Park. But he works hard, and is happy.

And me.

I wrote a novel, my first one, about an RC salesman, and something about the life he leads, the way his work and love intersect, for better and worse. And because the main character in that novel feels for his job a certain disdain, a certain distance between himself and what he does, my father believes I have a certain disdain for him and for what he has done all these years.

I believe he thinks, finally, that all that RC stuff has been for nought, given the outcomes of the lives of his sons, none of them in the business, none of them having panned out as he may have planned, all those thousands-of-cases-sold ago, way back on a morning when his children believed the entire endeavor—Royal Crown—to be only a game.

It would be easy for me simply to say, here and now, that this is not true, to give only words, in written form, to the contrary of what he has said to me face-to-face before: "You think working for RC was a waste." But I think it better to say that while I wrote that first book I got up at five-fifteen each morning, long before daylight, and wrote, in me some natural rhythm begun by no one other than him. Even now I am the first one up in our household, though I allow myself to sleep in, rise at six, a luxury after all those years; and I spend my days at work here, in this room, my office, where there sits on a file cabinet an old RC 16-ounce bottle, the diamond-and-crown logo in red and white on the glass, the same bottle I might have carried all those years ago across our front lawn and to the curb, now a totem that speaks to me of the value of work.

Some mornings I trek half an hour from here to an independent donut stand, not one of those chains, just for the reasonable facsimile of a bear claw.

It starts as a game, three boys pouring sodas down the gutter, watching colors swirl up, brandishing empties once the soda is poured out, their father waiting for them in the garage, more bottles to empty, more soda to spill, more fun to be had.

And it occurs to me only now, me a parent, the father of two boys whose histories lie before us all, unknown jobs and unknown people and unknown events all waiting to move upon them in whatever way this world moves in all our lives; it only occurs to me now that my father's examples of skill with a broom, with revving an engine for me, with sharing the communion meal of Cornnuts and M&M's together, even him coming into my room before daylight and calling out my name in his deep and solid voice, then the words "Time to get up," all of these, I know only now, were his attempts to guide me and my brothers the only way he knew how, all of these my father's effort to hold on to Brad and to Tim and to me, to keep us there with him, all uttered in the only language he knew: Royal Crown, and its presence in his life, his focus, his own anchor.

It ends with no end at all, of course, as we are all still alive, still here. And here are only permutations, variations on the themes of work and love, all our lives splintered away from intention and desire, from will and choice, to reveal the influence, finally, of Royal Crown: four men at work, living, providing, going on.

Mornings

Jacob and I walk the dog in the morning.

I walk, he rides his bike.

I'd been walking the dog alone each morning at six for a few weeks, ever since I met with a doctor who told me to get exercise.

Then one morning I opened our bedroom door on my way downstairs, found Jacob standing there, dressed for the day in his shorts and T-shirt and white socks. I looked past him, saw through the sliver of open door that his bed was already made.

He said, "Can I go with you?" He stood with his hands behind his back, seemed to twist in the smallest way, his eyes on mine.

I said, "Sure."

With these words our pact was made, our partnership formed.

———

We get up now at the same time, put our tennis shoes on out in the garage, the two of us sitting next to each other on the last step down from the kitchen door. Then I slip the leash on the dog, roll up the garage door, and we are off.

Sometimes it's foggy out here, our home so close to the water; sometimes it's hot, the air thick already, bugs out, dew dripping off the eaves of the house. But we walk the dog.

Jake is careful not to go too far ahead of me or lag too far behind. He rides his bike in circles on the street, or in figure eights, or in long, straight lines four or five houses down; then turns around, races back. The streets here are empty this early, only one or two cars passing us each morning. Each time one shows up Jake pulls to the right, slows down, watches out.

We talk. "In Spanish yesterday Tyrone threw up on the carpet," he tells me as he circles a patched pothole; "Zeb went into my room without asking," he says as he tries steering the bike by holding the center of the handlebar with one hand; "Clams have a foot," he says, and coasts, his feet off the pedals, toes dragging on the ground.

I give him no instruction, only claim not to have known about that foot, agree that entering his room without permission is truly a breach of conduct, express hope that Tyrone is feeling better, and tell him of a kid who threw up in my math class in high school, all over somebody's desk. We laugh, of course.

Each morning we follow one of three or four circuits through the neighborhood. This is an older neighborhood, though our house is new here, built on a tract of land opened up not long ago. But the houses around us have been here awhile, so our walks take us along streets dense with wax myrtle and magnolia, dogwood and wisteria, Savannah holly and dwarf gardenia, honeysuckle and hibiscus; lawns accented with vinca and lantana and day lilies, framed in redtips and ligustrum and compacta holly. Live oaks thick with Spanish moss loom over us; pine trees poke high up into the morning air, pinecones littered beneath them like lost prayers.

For Jake all of these are occasions for comment about colors, or smells, or, even, eating. He stops his bike at a mailbox shrouded with honeysuckle in bloom, pops off a flower, expertly guides the filament from inside the petals, then puts it to his mouth, licks it. "Honeysuckle," he says to me, and pops off another flower. "People eat it." He finishes with this flower, pulls off the next. "We do this at recess," he says.

"Oh," I say, and pass him, the dog leading me on. "I did that when I was a kid," I say over my shoulder. "We had honeysuckle in our backyard."

"Really?" he says, and climbs back on the bike, finished.

Another morning he says, "Look at those roses," as we near the house on the corner of Bampfield and East Hobcaw, a house whose front yard is taken up by a rose garden as big as a basketball court. He stops, his feet on either side of the bike, his hands on the handlebars.

He says, "There's all colors in there." He pauses, and I reach him, pass him, the dog eager, as always, to keep going, keep going.

"There's pink, and red. Violet. Purple." He stops, says from behind me, "There's blue roses in there, too."

"Oh?" I say. "I didn't know there was such a thing as blue roses."

Now he moves past me, slowly pedals the bike, his eyes to the road ahead. "I think there's blue ones," he says, and moves on.

Each circuit is different, but each delivers us, finally, down one or another street that dead-ends on the marsh and Hobcaw Creek, out past it the Wando. The sun rises over the creeks so that silver light shines off fingers of water reaching into the marsh, sharp edges of light inside the saw grass and yellowgrass and saltmarsh hay. These are our endpoints, where we turn around, head back toward home, Zeb and Melanie already having begun breakfast back there: Eggo waffles or grits and sausage or omelettes or simply bowls of cereal, pieces of toast.

This morning we take the circuit that delivers us to the end of Coinbow. Jake makes it there first, sits on his bike, toes just touching the ground. His back is to me, his bike aimed at the water as though he will simply ride off over it all.

I reach the end of the street, see before us the marsh and the creek. A thin mist hangs in the light, a mist that makes the live oak and pine across the creek seem like ghost sentinels, ancient and distant and just beyond reach. Still, the sun sifts through the mist to give us that same silver light on water, brilliant reflections too sharp to look at for long.

"It's beautiful," I say as I round the end of the street, the dog still leading, and already I am heading home, back toward where Coinbow and Bampfield intersect. Then it's left onto Bampfield, left onto Isaw, right onto Lackland, and home.

"Yep," he says.

I look behind me, see he sits there a moment longer, toes still touching the ground. I see out past him the marsh, the water, that mist, my son inside it all.

Then he backs up the bike, turns the handlebars, starts pedaling. A moment later he moves past me, feet moving fast. "Watch me," he says, and picks up speed. He leans forward, over the handlebars: his racing mode.

This is my second son, my younger child.

What I know is this: He is seven and a half. He loves his bike. He is in first grade and has made principal's list all three quarters. His best friend's name is Garrett, and they fight like brothers. He weighs seventy-three pounds, stands four feet, four and a half inches as of three weeks ago Tuesday, and can run a mile in seven minutes. He goes through tennis shoes quicker than anyone I have ever known.

And he accompanies me each morning with no prodding, the only pact between us the few words exchanged that first morning, when he asked if he could come.

This is my second son, my younger child. There will be no more after him. This is what I know.

He makes it to the end of Coinbow, a good five or six houses up, then wheels his bike around toward me, starts pedaling again, leans forward over the handlebars, picks up speed.

"Watch me," he says again as he nears me, racing down Coinbow, back toward the marsh, that light, and in that moment I reach my free hand out, intend to tousle his hair as he pedals past.

Here he is, my hand out, and I say, "There's the Jaybo!"

But my hand does not touch his head, his hair passing just beneath my fingers, my son moves so swiftly, and all I am left with is an instant of air, the rush of it in my hand, the draft created by a boy moving this fast.

Not enough, but all I have.